The Digital Die

Today's Digital Tools in Small L

21st Century Fluency Project

Andrew Churches

Andrew Churches is a teacher and ICT enthusiast. He teaches at Kristin School on Auckland's North Shore, a school with a mobile computing program that sees students with personal mobile devices and laptops. He is an edublogger, wiki author, and innovator. In 2008, Andrew's wiki, Educational Origami, was nominated for the Edublogs Best Wiki awards. He contributes to a number of web sites and blogs including Techlearning, Spectrum Education magazine, and the Committed Sardine Blog. Andrew believes that to prepare our students for the future we must prepare them for change and teach them to question, think, adapt, and modify.

Lee Crockett

Lee Crockett is a national award-winning designer, marketing consultant, entrepreneur, artist, author, and international keynote speaker. He is the director of media for the InfoSavvy Group and the managing partner of the 21st Century Fluency Project. Lee is a "just in time learner" who is constantly adapting to the new programs, languages, and technologies associated with today's communications and marketing media. Understanding the need for balance in our increasingly digital lives, Lee has lived in Kyoto, Japan, where he studied Aikido and the tea ceremony, as well as Florence, Italy, where he studied painting at the Accademia D'Arte.

Ian Jukes

Ian Jukes is the founder and director of the InfoSavvy Group, an international consulting firm. He has been a teacher at all grade levels; a school, district, and provincial administrator; a university instructor; and a national and international consultant. But first and foremost Ian is a passionate educational evangelist. To date he has written or co-written 12 books and 9 educational series and has had more than 200 articles published in various journals around the world. From the beginning, Ian's focus has been on the compelling need to restructure our educational institutions so that they become relevant to the current and future needs of children or, as David Thornburg writes, "to prepare them for their future and not just our past." That's why his materials tend to focus on the many pragmatic issues that provide the essential context for educational restructuring.

21st Century Fluency Project

co-published with

CORWIN
A SAGE Company

For information:

21st Century Fluency Project Inc.
1685 Smithson Place
Kelowna BC Canada V1Y 8N5

www.21stcenturyfluency.com

ISBN 1-4499-7550-X (pbk.)
EAN 9781449975500

Acquisitions Editor: Debra Stollenwerk
Editorial, Production, and Indexing: Abella Publishing Services, LLC
Typesetter: Ross Crockett
Cover Designer: Lee Crockett

I would like to acknowledge the patience and support of my family —Tania, Brooke, Nathaniel & Jayden—who have put up with me being distracted and busy as we developed the book; as well as for their encouragement to keep trying when things became difficult. I also want to acknowledge my students at Kristin School, who have been a constant source of inspiration and ideas; as well as my long-suffering friends and colleagues, who proofread the chapters, and allowed themselves to be used as sounding boards for my ideas. Their excellent ideas, imagination, creativity and encouragement helped make this book possible.

Andrew Churches

I dedicate this book to my mom. Shouldn't everyone dedicate a book to their mother? She is an inspiration, someone who believes that when we stop learning we stop living, that no matter how much we know there is more that we don't know, and that curiosity ensures humility. Mom, here's your tech support manual.

Lee Crockett

This book is dedicated to my Dad, Arthur Hamilton Jukes, who left us far too quickly; to my stepmom Marion, who with grace, elegance and quiet determination carries forward the memory of my Father; to my sisters Ann and Cathy and my brother John, who were of great support during difficult times; to my sons Kyler and Kolby, who are living proof that the flame still burns; and to my New Zealand friend Nicky Mohan, who has helped me understand that friendship is only a Skype call away.

Ian Jukes

Many thanks to Tania Sullivan, Helen Mansfield, Doug De Kock, Tomomi Watanabe, Dr. Jason Ohler, Sandra McLeroy, Brad Biehn, Karen Boyes, Shari Camhi, Nicky Mohan, Ross Crockett, Dr. James Cisek, Deb Stollenwerk, Mick Harper, Leigh Peake, Belinda Thresher, Mae Crockett and Lori Anderson

Table of Contents

The 21st Century Fluency Project

Foreword

Introduction

21st Century Fluency Project

The 21st Century Fluency Project is about moving vision into practice through the process of investigating the effect of the last few decades on our society and particularly on our children, learning how we in education must adapt, and, finally, committing to meaningful changes at the classroom level.

The Digital Diet is the third book in our 21st Century Fluency Series. Its purpose is to help familiarize you with some of the different ways we are interacting and connecting in the online world, and with some of the most popular and efficient tools designed for these purposes.

A series of books, as well as related supporting materials, have been developed in order to answer five essential questions that teachers will ask when considering how educators and education must respond to the profound developments that are being experienced in the world at large. These questions are:

Why do I have to change?

Living on the Future Edge
The Impact of Global Exponential Trends on Education in the 21st Century

In this book, we discuss the power of paradigm to shape our thinking, the pressure that technological development is putting on our paradigm for teaching and learning, six global exponential trends in technological development that we can't ignore, what each of these trends means for education, new skills for students, new roles for teachers, and scenarios of education in the future.

Understanding the Digital Generation
Teaching and Learning in the New Digital Landscape

This book examines the effects that digital bombardment from constant exposure to electronic media has on children in the new digital landscape, and considers the profound implications this holds for the future of education. What does the latest neuroscientific and psychological research tell us about the role of intense and frequent experiences on the brain, particularly the young and impressionable brain?

Based on the research, what inferences can we make about children's digital experiences and how these experiences are rewiring and reshaping their cognitive processes? More important, what are the implications for teaching, learning, and assessment in the new digital landscape?

How can we reconcile these new developments with current instructional practices, particularly in a climate of standards and accountability driven by high-stakes testing for all? What strategies can we use to appeal to the learning preferences and communication needs of digital learners while at the same time honoring our traditional assumptions and practices related to teaching, learning, and assessment?

Where do I start?

The Digital Diet
Today's Digital Tools in Small Bytes

This book offers bite-sized, progressively challenging projects to introduce the reader to the digital landscape of today. This is the world of our children and students. *The Digital Diet* will help readers shed pounds of assumptions and boost their digital metabolism to help keep pace with these kids by learning to use some simple yet powerful digital tools.

How can I teach differently?

Teaching for Tomorrow
Teaching Content and Problem-Solving Skills

A key book in this series, *Teaching for Tomorrow* is a practical book for teachers struggling with how to teach 21st-century problem-solving skills while, at the same time, still covering the content in the curriculum guide. The book outlines a new teaching approach that significantly shifts the roles of the teacher and the student in learning. These new roles facilitate student ownership of learning. *Teaching for Tomorrow* also outlines the 4D problem-solving process, a process that students learn to use effectively as they become independent problem solvers.

What would this teaching look like in my classroom?

Literacy Is Not Enough
21st Century Fluencies for the Digital Age

It is no longer enough that we educate only to the standards of the traditional literacies of the 20th century. To be competent and capable in the 21st century requires a completely different set of skills above and beyond traditional literacies. These are the 21st-century fluencies that are identified and explained in detail in this book. The balance of the book introduces our framework for integrating these fluencies in our traditional curriculum and outlines a planning tool that can be used by educators to create their own 21st-century learning unit.

Curriculum Integration Kits

These kits are subject- and grade-specific publications designed to integrate the teaching of the 21st-century fluencies into today's curriculum and classroom. Included are detailed learning scenarios, resources, rubrics, and lesson plans with suggestions for high-tech, low-tech, or no-tech implementation. Also identified is the traditional content covered, as well as the standards and 21st-century fluencies each project covers.

The 21st Century Fluency Project web site
www.21stcenturyfluency.com

Our web site contains supplemental material that provides support for classroom teachers who are implementing 21st-century teaching. The site provides teachers with access to pre-made lesson plans that teach traditional content along with 21st-century fluencies. The site also offers teachers an online writing tool for designing their own lessons and teaching 21st-century fluencies, as well as other shared resources and a forum for additional collaboration and support.

How can we design effective schools for the 21st century?

Teaching the Digital Generation
No More Cookie Cutter High Schools

The world has changed. Young people have changed. But the same underlying assumptions about teachers, students, and instruction that have guided high school design for a hundred years continue to shape the way high schools are designed today. In fact, so much is assumed about the way a high school should look, that new schools continue to be created from a long-established template that is used without question. Strip away the skylights, the fancy foyers, and the high-tech P.A. systems, and most new schools being constructed today look pretty much the way they did when most adults went to school. This is a mismatch with reality. We need new designs that incorporate what we have learned about young people and how they learn best. This book outlines a new process for designing high schools and provides descriptions of several new models for how schools can be configured to better support learning.

Foreword

Welcome to *The Digital Diet*. Over the course of the past several years I have been involved in the creation of more than a dozen books and educational resources. Without question, the writing of *The Digital Diet* has been one of the most amazing experiences I have ever had. That's why I am absolutely honored to write the foreword to this book. But as extraordinary as the book is, the process by which it was created is even more so. Let me explain.

A few of years back, I made a spotlight presentation in a crowded hall at the National Education Computing Conference (NECC) in San Antonio, Texas. As I hurriedly packed to make way for the next speaker, I was approached by a man with a strange speech impediment (although others would call that impediment an accent). This was of course Andrew Churches from Auckland, New Zealand. After a very brief introduction, Andrew launched into a description of some quite remarkable work he was doing on moving Bloom's Taxonomy into the Digital Age. In total, we spent about five minutes talking and until recently, that was the only time that Andrew and I had spoken face to face. Despite the fact that Andrew and his family live on the other side of the planet, we became fast friends. I know his children by name as they know mine, I know his wife (she has my deepest sympathies), and I have literally spent hundreds of hours talking and waxing effluent with Andrew via Skype.

Andrew Churches is, at his core, a consummate professional—a classroom teacher with an outstanding understanding of a wide range of academic and non-academic fields. He is a scientist, technologist, outdoorsman, environmentalist, leader in the International Baccalaureate program, highly respected speaker, award-winning blogger, and a passionate advocate for the need to fundamentally transform education. In his personal life, he is a loving and extraordinarily patient parent to his children, and partner to his long-suffering wife.

I met Lee Crockett in a completely different way. For many years now, I have worked on the second floor of an old department store that has been converted into offices and a studio. One of the other original tenants was Lee. Through happenstance we became acquaintances, friends, and eventually colleagues. Lee is an award-winning designer, marketing consultant, entrepreneur, artist, sailor, motorcycle racer, musician, restauranteur, and writer who has lived and worked in several countries. Lee is the absolute essence of the 21st-century thinker and a "just-in-time learner," who is constantly adapting to the new programs, languages, and technologies associated with today's digital communications and marketing media.

A consistent theme in my presentations is the need for older generations to embrace the digital culture. We need to make a concerted effort to get comfortable with the digital tools our children spend so much of their time with, and bring these tools to the classroom. It is my passionate belief that doing this can keep learning relevant to the only person that matters—the learner. In my travels and work, which typically take me to more than half a dozen countries a year, I am consistently confronted by a problem: Those of us not born into the digital culture just don't know where to begin. This is completely understandable. Even for people like Andrew and Lee, who eat this stuff for breakfast, lunch, and dinner, have a hard time keeping up with the digital landscape! The questions consistently asked of me by teachers include "Where do I begin? How do I use these tools personally? How do I use them in my classroom?"

My response to these questions is "How do you eat an elephant?" The answer of course, is one bite at a time." Or in this case one "byte" at a time. I had spent a great deal of time thinking about how to create a digital diet—a diet that would allow new learners to consider one new thing each week. When I ran my idea of creating a digital diet for white-knuckle technology users by Andrew and Lee, they jumped in with both feet. Of course, as the saying goes, "Beauty is in the eyes of the beerholder," so each of them came at the idea of a digital diet from a very different perspective. And this book is the result.

Diets don't provide immediate results. Rather, diets that work require lifelong changes in daily habits. Effective diets make gradual, sustainable changes that take dieters to their goals in small steps. And that's exactly what this book promotes—A digital diet. This is not a diet that will bring about instant change but rather a series of small steps that will support you as you explore and learn about the amazing digital world we live in.

I can't think of a simpler or more comfortable way to learn about the digital landscape than to commit to your own digital diet. Andrew and Lee have provided a simple map to help show the way.

It's not the only map by any means, but it's a compelling one that help you begin the journey to embracing and incorporating powerful tools into your teaching, your professional learning, and your personal life. The challenge is up to you. How will you use this map? What will you see, and how will you respond when you gaze at the digital landscape that stands in front of us? Most important, what concrete actions will you take as a result of reading this book?

Ian Jukes, March 2010

 Introduction

> The Internet is the single most important development in the history of human communications since the invention of "call waiting."
>
> **Dave Barry, in *Dave Barry in Cyberspace* (1996), p. 121**

Virtually—A Different Way to Collaborate

In *Living on the Future Edge* (2010), we discussed the global exponential trends that are altering the very fabric of our society. The explosion of technological power and bandwidth has caused the death of distance. As Thomas Friedman says, "The world is flat." Distance has never meant less than it does today.

This book is proof of that, and we wanted to share with you the process of its development.

In 2008, Ian was presenting at NECC in San Antonio. After his talk, Andrew introduced himself. Their conversation lasted only a few minutes. Over the course of the next few months, they exchanged several emails. Andrew shared some of his writing and the amazing work he had been doing in New Zealand. Immediately, Ian saw that Andrew was a like-minded character who fit perfectly into our group.

At the time, Lee was living in Italy. On one of their daily Skype video chats, Ian told Lee about this crazy Kiwi he'd met at NECC and how he thought the three of them should write a book together. That was the beginning of this project.

A few months later, Lee met Andrew for the first time—not in person, but on Skype. Through three-way video chats and follow-up emails, the idea for *The Digital Diet* and several other projects took form.

When it came time to write the book, the three authors started working collaboratively through Adobe Buzzword. Whenever one of them logged in and worked on a chapter, they could see who else had been working on it and exactly what the changes had been.

Over the winter and spring, they all got to know each other pretty well. Though they had never met in person, Lee had met Andrew's children, seen his home, visited his classroom, and watched him interact with his students—all by video chat.

Think about this for a moment. This book was written on the Internet. It never existed on anyone's computer during the writing process. It was never printed out. And it was written by three people, in three different parts of the world, who had never been together physically in the same place, yet virtually sat down in the same room together.

While the collaborative writing process took place through video chat and online tools, personal relationships were also being developed through the same media.

Does this sound like science fiction to you? Do your friends and colleagues appear to be speaking in strange languages? Have you heard them say, "You should be on Facebook" or "I just tweeted Ryan," and you are left wondering what they are talking about? Do people ask you if you have Skype or a blog or if you share your pictures using Flickr? Do you get the sense that there's something going on and that you are being left behind and missing out? Do you feel like you just can't catch up to hundreds if not thousands of different digital tools and technologies that seem to be appearing every day? Does it appear that your friends are speaking in tongues or need to have their medication increased?

If you answered yes to any of these questions, then this is the book for you!

What Is a Digital Diet?

We have all heard of radical diets that promise everything and deliver little. Some will cut out all fats, others will cut out all carbohydrates, still others will have you eat a tiny range of foods, and others will have you eat fillers that set like Jell-O in your stomach and fool you into feeling full and satisfied. But the common thing about most diets is they are not sustainable.

You can't lose 30 pounds of ugly fat in two weeks if it has taken you years to get to that state. An effective diet is one that is going to make lifelong changes and is not a radical, quick-fix diet. It's a diet that makes gradual, sustainable changes. It's a diet that takes you to the goals you want to achieve in small steps.

This is a digital diet. It is not designed to make instant change. Rather, a digital diet outlines a series of steps that will support you as you explore and investigate the amazing digital world we live in. You can't change the habits of a lifetime in an instant. This is the mistake many traditional diets make. Instead you have to gradually explore taking the steps that suit you and at the pace that meets your needs. In much the same way, you don't have to devour this book in one sitting. Rather, you should try to slowly enjoy each succulent chapter, sampling the delights that each step on your digital diet brings.

The digital diet approaches each chapter of the book by offering the following elements:

- *Clear goals and objectives*—This book is going to help you use a variety of great tools that will allow you to stay in touch with your friends and have fun. It will allow you to get the information you need easily and efficiently and save it so you can access it at any time from anywhere.

- *Skills*—This book will provide you with a step-by-step guide to setting up and using these new digital tools and technologies. Each chapter takes you through a series of small steps that show you how to use the tools and share the information you have.

- *Incentive*—Incentives are often useful to making change. No matter how good the ideas are, how fantastic the resources and user guides are, and how detailed your plan, you have to want to change. This book provides these incentives.

- *Resources*—This book will provide you with the resources and materials you need to understand the basics of each tool. Each chapter provides links to other online resources so you can expand your knowledge and expertise.

- *A plan*—This book is a step-by-step guide. But you don't have to do every thing! Too often diets require you to choreograph your life to the smallest step. This digital diet doesn't. If the tool or technology doesn't fit your interests and needs, then we suggest you don't use it!

- *Further exploration*—Links to additional resources are provided for those who might want to know a little bit more about the areas that are being profiled.

Where Do I Start?

In this book, we are going to look at all the steps and stages you need to use a selection of stable digital tools to enhance your use of the digital world. Chapter 1 looks at us as digital citizens. This chapter will take you through how to keep yourself, your friends, and your ideas safe while respecting others and their property.

In Chapters 2 and 3, we will look at how to find the information you want and then save it and share it with others. At the time of this writing, it is estimated there are more than 250 million web sites on the Internet. These two chapters will show you how to locate what you need when you need it.

Chapters 4, 7, 9, and 10 will look at different ways of sharing your resources. Whether it's showing your friends your holiday photos, writing an online diary, making a rich presentation of your voice and photographs, or using a short message to stay in touch, these chapters have it all.

Chapter 5 harnesses the power of the Internet to text, talk, and videoconference with your friends and colleagues for free! Using Skype, you can stay in touch no matter how near or far you are from your important people.

Chapter 6 introduces you to the world of Twitter. Twitter is a popular tool used for what is called "microblogging", and it's a whole new way of blogging and staying in touch with your friends and family.

In Chapter 8, we will dive into Facebook. Here you will take small and safe steps that will guide you through the phenomenon of our times—social networking.

In the appendix, we discuss email. Electronic mail is one of the core foundations of everyone's use of the digital world.

Do you have to read it from start to finish in sequence? No! Each chapter stands by itself. Read what suits you and try what sounds like fun in the sequence that feels right for you. Remember to take your time and be patient—this is fun, exciting stuff that can sometimes seem a little challenging. But the rewards are huge. Be patient, relax, and have a good time.

Ready?

Set?

Go!

Further Questions

- What are some of the technologies and digital tools you are using today that you weren't using 20 years ago?

- How have those technologies and tools changed your life during this period of time?

- What new technologies and tools have you heard of, but don't really know much about?

- What new technologies and tools are you interested in finding out more information about?

- Where would you go to find this information?

Resources

BBC Webwise—www.bbc.co.uk/webwise/course

Blog list for online digital tools—
http://literacyispriceless.wordpress.com/2009/12/07/digital-tools-for-homework-help

A list of digital media resources compiled by Gary S. Stager—
www.stager.org/imovie/index.html

DBookworm.com Digital Resource Center—http://dbookworm.com

Discovery Education classroom resources—http://school.discoveryeducation.com

Downloadable PDFs for building and assessing digital skills—
http://ltt.cdnis.edu.hk/files/pdf/articles/building_digital_skills.pdf and
www.atomicdog.com/PDF/Skills-CH05.pdf

Chapter 1
The Digital Citizen

> Our species needs, and deserves, a citizenry with minds wide awake and a basic understanding of how the world works.
>
> **Carl Sagan**

Expectations: What Will You Learn?

The Digital Citizen is an ethical and moral individual who considers his or her actions and their consequences. These individuals are aware of the risks and benefits of the unparalleled degree of access we have to information.

This chapter is the starting point for our journey of exploration and discovery. Here we will learn about protecting and respecting others and ourselves. We will explore real-world examples and contemplate how we can deal with some of these issues. We will consider intellectual property and alternatives to piracy. The goal of this chapter is not to frighten or scare you, but rather to raise an awareness of both the positive and negative aspects of the Internet.

Digital Citizen Terminology

Flaming is when a person publicly attacks or "outs" a person. This can often be a series of posts or comments using discussion boards and forums or chatrooms and instant messaging.

Discussion boards are a web space where users can post or write comments. These can be restricted to only members of the space or open to the public. Many discussion boards or forums are moderated.

Moderation is the process of approving comments or posts by a moderator. Once approved, other users can see the comments or posts.

Posts are comments, statements, articles, or presentations published by a user. The term *post* covers blog entries (see Chapter 7), short messages using tools such as Twitter (see Chapter 6), email messages to discussion boards or forums, or updates on a social networking site (see Chapter 8).

Spam is unsolicited or unrequested email often sent by fictitious companies. Spam is a huge issue creating vast email traffic and causing great annoyance.

Piracy is the illegal copying and/or distribution of copyrighted materials. This can include music, images, movies, television programs, written works, and other intellectual property.

Predator is a person using the Internet and online social mediums to groom, stalk, and make contact with a goal of sexual exploitation.

Grooming is a technique used by predators to select and prepare a person for meeting the predator. This technique involves building a degree of trust between the victim and the predator.

Cyberbullying is the process of attacking and bullying a person using electronic mediums such as email, instant messaging, discussion boards, cell phones, and so on.

Bloggers are the authors of blogs, or web logs (see Chapter 7).

Phishing is a technique used to gain personal and private information. Usually phishing occurs when you receive an email from an apparently legitimate source asking you to provide information or to link to a web site to update your personal information. The information that is collected (such as bank account or credit card details) is used by the email or web site authors.

Malware is a term used to describe malicious software. This can include viruses, trojans, adware, spyware, and so on.

Open source software (OSS) is software, often produced by a community of developers, that is freely available for use and often for distribution. OSS can be modified, as the source code is open to view and change.

Profile is the personal information that is entered in social networking (see Chapter 8) and other sites.

Tenets of Digital Citizenship

In Rome, to be a citizen was a goal to aspire to. A Roman citizen was exempt from some charges, protected against certain punishments, and empowered with rights such as voting, making contracts, marriage, and standing for office. But with these rights also came responsibilities. The citizen of Rome had to:

- speak Latin
- pay taxes
- serve jury duty
- be registered and identified by birth certificate and census
- uphold social responsibilities and be seen as virtuous

To be a digital citizen has similar benefits and responsibilities. A good digital citizen will experience the advantages of the digital world and, like the Roman citizen, will also be identifiable, speak using the appropriate language, serve his or her duty to judge what is appropriate within the laws of the land and ethical behavior, uphold their social responsibilities, and be virtuous.

The Internet is a little like the proverbial elephant that never forgets. Our digital footprints are not like the footprints on the beach, washed away by the next wave or rising tide. Rather, they are like footprints left to dry in the wet concrete of the footpath—permanent.

The digital citizen needs to follow six tenets of citizenship:

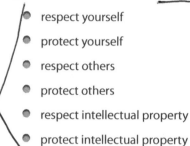

- respect yourself
- protect yourself
- respect others
- protect others
- respect intellectual property
- protect intellectual property

Respect Yourself

This means being a virtuous citizen. It is too easy to present yourself in an unflattering or even inappropriate manner. Respecting yourself starts with the name you use to present yourself online. How often do we see social networking or Twitter names that are suggestive, questionable, or downright crude? How about the images posted to social sites that are provocative, revealing, or less than flattering? Not respecting yourself can come back to haunt you. Increasingly, employers are searching social networking sites to research potential employees.

How do your profile, online name, and image portray you as the potential member of a professional organization?

Many of the social sites will also ask you to comment on your sexual orientation, relationship status, experimentation with drugs, and, in more extreme cases, your sexual activities or preferences. You need to consider the potential outcomes of revealing these aspects of your life to what is increasingly a public forum. While many social networking sites do have privacy options, the default level of access could allow others to see your most personal and intimate information accessible via applications (such as tools created in social networks that access your profile) or via your friends, their friends, or associates.

Recommendations

- *Select names and images that portray you in a positive light.*
- *Do not post any information that you would not want your mother, grandparent, or employer to see.*
- *Leave questions about your relationships, experimentation with drugs, sexual activities, preferences, or other such personal information blank.*

Use ethical approaches such as:

- *I will show respect for myself through my actions.*
- *I will select online names that are appropriate.*
- *I will consider the information and images I intend to use before I post online.*
- *I will consider what personal information about my life, experiences, experimentation, and relationships I post.*
- *I will not be obscene.*

Protect Yourself

Sometimes even innocent things can hold the potential of unintended and unexpected consequences. A few years ago, I had my attention drawn to a social networking page of a student. The page was not inappropriate or obscene; it did not contain references to sex or drugs or even "rock 'n roll." The student was a bright and bubbly 12-year-old girl, interested in horses, skiing, and having fun. She was sharing with her friends and her profile was public. The information she posted was innocent, but in her naivete she had posted images of herself dressed only in her bikini, together with a "week in–week out" schedule of her activities, such as, ". . . every Tuesday I ride at the pony club and on Wednesday I am skiing at Snow Planet."

Unintentionally, she had provided any potential predator with a profile of herself, complete with information about where to meet her, along with some conversation starters about her interests, hobbies, friends, and music. The young girl had done nothing inappropriate; she was simply open and trusting. She was naive, as you would expect of a young child. However, the consequences could be devastating.

Adults do not fare much better. Open statements about your sexual orientation can bring about social isolation, cyberbullying, and potentially physical assaults. In many cultures, you risk prosecution or persecution by announcing that you are of a different faith, are not heterosexually oriented, support a particular political party, or hold strong opinions about some matter.

For this reason, you need to consider what you write. And this caution is not just limited to social networking sites. Blogs, wikis, Twitter, YouTube, and instant messaging services also allow you to express your opinions.

While some countries uphold the rights of freedom of speech, this is not the case in all nations around the world. In some countries, there is potential risk for venturing to publish views and opinions that are contrary to the doctrine of the ruling parties. As we have seen in China, North Korea, Myanmar, and more recently in Iran, expressing your opposition can be a danger to you and your family.

The rise of citizen journalism, where bloggers, tweets, and wiki authors report newsworthy events via these mediums, has also led to other risks, not the least of which is prosecution for defamation. It pays to be sure of your facts before you publish. No matter how passionate you are about a topic, or how big you perceive the injustice to be, discretion is the better part of valor.

Many of us will, at some stage, find ourselves the target of bullying or online abuse. If this does happen, it's crucial that you don't try to deal with it on your own. Tell someone you trust—a friend, parent, teacher, employer, or counselor. Report the abuse to the moderator of the site. Don't respond to it. Record it for evidence.

In 2007, Oxford Internet Surveys' *Internet in Britain* report found that almost 12 percent of Internet users have met an online acquaintance offline. The Internet provides a great medium to meet new people and develop new friendships, but it is crucial that this is done with an awareness of the nature of the Internet. The public profile a person puts forward may be a facade of lies that hides the true person behind it. In the United States, it is reported that one in eight marriages in 2008 started with an online relationship. Social media has huge potential for establishing new relationships but does have a similar potential for risk.

Recommendations

- *Think about the information you are posting. What will it mean to an outsider viewing it? What will it mean without the prior information your audience (friends, blog subscribers, Twitter followers, and so on) may have?*

- *Don't publish a schedule of your activities.*

- *Set the privacy settings on your tools to control access to your updates, posts, or profile.*

- *Be sure of the facts you post.*

- *Remember this adage: "Send in haste, repent at leisure."*

- *It's easy to send an email or post a message in a moment of passion or impulsiveness, but once sent, it's almost impossible to delete. Think before you post.*

Use ethical approaches such as:

- *I will ensure the information, images, and materials I post online will not put me at risk.*

- *I will not publish my personal details, contact details, or a schedule of my activities.*

- *I will report any attacks or inappropriate behavior directed at me.*

- *I will protect passwords, accounts, and resources.*

- *If I am meeting someone in the real world that I have met online, I will discuss it with people I trust, such as parents, colleagues, or friends, and never meet them alone.*

Respect Others

As a responsible cyber or digital citizen, we model respect for other people. In the past, gossip was limited to your immediate field of friends and acquaintances, but with the advent and uptake of digital technologies, the potential audience for gossip and innuendo is global. The ease with which anyone with Internet access can publish is incredible. Publishing in a digital medium is as simple as typing or speaking. As you will read in Chapter 7, anyone can set up and publish a blog in a matter of minutes with the potential of an immense audience.

Being disrespectful online is called *flaming*. Among many possible examples, flaming could involve writing a post or thread or uploading a YouTube video that attacks a person. A good general rule to follow is this: if you wouldn't say it in person, don't say it online.

Respect for others goes beyond the material we might publish. It includes the sites we visit. Whether it is gossip, hate, racism, or pornography, we should be discerning because by visiting, we give our tacit approval for sites such as these to exist.

In particular, the pornography industry is one of the saddest in the world. According to a range of estimates, upwards of 12 percent of all web sites and hundreds of millions of porn pages generate billions of dollars in revenue annually. Beneath its facade of ecstatic pleasure lies persecution, desperation, abuse, hopelessness, sadness, and despair. How many young children have been drawn into these sordid scenes in order to make enough money to survive? Does the sex industry portray real human relationships? Do the eyes of the models show passion or sorrow?

Recommendations

- *If you have nothing nice to say, then say nothing.*
- *If it's inappropriate or questionable, don't forward it, don't visit it, and don't condone it.*
- *Teach and talk about real relationships.*

Use ethical approaches such as:

- *I will show respect to others.*
- *I will not use electronic mediums to flame, bully, harass, or stalk other people.*
- *I will show respect for other people in my choice of web sites.*
- *I will not visit sites that are degrading, pornographic, racist, or inappropriate.*
- *I will not abuse my rights of access or enter other people's private spaces or areas without permission.*

Protect Others

As digital citizens, we have a duty to protect other people. We can't stand idly by watching bullying or abuse and breathe a sigh of relief that it is not us who are the targets. We can't accept flaming, bullying, or inappropriate behavior. And we certainly can't sit idly by and watch others suffer. By sitting by quietly as a person is flamed in a threaded discussion, or attacked by a troll in a chatroom, we encourage the attacker and validate their position. You cannot sit by and let such behavior continue.

Every social networking site, instant messaging tool, chatroom, wiki, blog, and social medium has a "report abuse" contact. USE IT! We can protect others by not ignoring abuse and reporting behavior that is inappropriate or unacceptable.

Don't forward emails that are derogatory—delete them. If the conversation in a chatroom changes and begins to have sexual or sinister overtones, report it. If you are not the target, it may be one of your friends. Consider what it would feel like if you were the recipient of such activity.

Recommendations

- *Have a policy of zero tolerance for unacceptable behavior. Report abuse.*
- *Don't forward unacceptable material—delete it. Stop the trail at your trashcan.*
- *Consider the other person's feelings and act accordingly.*

Use ethical approaches such as:

- *I will protect others by reporting abuse.*
- *I will not forward inappropriate materials or communications.*
- *I will not visit sites that are degrading, pornographic, racist, or inappropriate.*

Respect Intellectual Property

There is so much information out there, and there are so many amazing materials to share. Many individuals have given of their precious time for free to create these resources. This final facet of good digital citizenship is to respect or honor intellectual property. Honoring intellectual property is not hard and requires little more than common courtesy, such as:

- citing the source of images and information
- giving credit when credit is due
- asking permission before you use resources
- linking to web sites rather than downloading and reposting
- sharing your own materials

Recommendations

- *Always seek permission before using information or media.*
- *Always cite information sources appropriately.*
- *Respect the authors' rights to not allow use of their works.*
- *Lead by example and share your own work.*

Use ethical approaches such as:

- *I will request permission to use resources.*
- *I will suitably cite any and all use of web sites, books, media, and so on.*
- *I will validate information.*
- *I will use and abide by the fair use rules.*

Protect Intellectual Property

The term *piracy* conjures up ideas of sailing ships, eye patches, and swashbuckling adventure. However, the reality of piracy is simple—PIRACY IS THEFT!

No matter what face you put on it, no matter whether it is software, music, or movies, PIRACY is THEFT! It is not acceptable to say that the movie industry, bands and artists, or software producers such as Microsoft's Bill Gates or Apple's Steve Jobs make enough money, so it doesn't matter. The simple reality is that without people purchasing the movies, music, or software, these companies would not exist, and our world would be poorer for the loss of their songs, films, and programs.

BitTorrent, LimeWire, and Kazaa have made the theft of music, movies, and programs as simple as clicking a mouse. Most of us would never consider walking into a video store and stealing a DVD. Yet we use programs that do exactly that. The impact of piracy is often seen to be distant and excused by comments such as, "Well, they are paid millions for that," but piracy costs the recording artists and software producers billions of dollars each year, and it discourages creativity and increases prices. Piracy takes away the opportunity for emerging artists to succeed.

It also has an effect in your own neighborhood—it directly decreases employment. When movies or music are stolen by being downloaded, your local music or video store loses sales, and this undermines the viability of the business and the livelihoods of the owner and employees.

There are alternatives. The Creative Commons licensing agreements have made available millions of images, masses of media, and libraries of books that are available, accessible, and free.

It is worth considering when you publish your works to use the Creative Commons license. Creative Commons is a license or statement of use that encourages people to share. Under the Creative Commons license, you can set the level of rights a user has to your intellectual property. Visit creativecommons.org to find out more.

Recommendations

- Use media and software within the limits of the licence or copyright agreement.
- Use alternative tools produced under Creative Commmons or Free and Open Source software.
- Acknowledge authors' rights and efforts by suitable citation.
- Remove media that has not been ethically obtained.
- License your works under appropriate licensing agreements.

Use ethical approaches such as:

- I will request to use the software and media others produce.
- I will use free and open-source alternatives rather than pirating software.
- I will purchase, license, and register all software.
- I will purchase my music and media, and I will refrain from distributing these in a manner that violates their licenses.
- I will act with integrity.

Summary

- As teachers, we are role models for appropriate behavior, and our influence on our students is huge and life spanning. Our students are entering a world where everything is available for them at the touch of their keyboard and the click of a mouse. If we can establish suitable processes and behaviors of digital citizenship, then they will have a solid foundation of ethical practice to base their future actions and interactions on.

- Digital citizens are self-aware and respect and protect others. They consider their actions and the impacts of these actions. They are aware of people, software developers, actors, artists and their agents, and agencies' rights to own and distribute media and gain a living from it. They respect these rights.

- With freedom comes responsibility.

Questions to Ask

- In keeping with the moral standard for having a personal online profile, how are you representing yourself in online domains, using mediums such as imagery and text? How do you represent yourself to others who see your profiles?

- How do you treat others as you contribute thought and opinion to public outlets like blogs and wall posts (Facebook) and tweets (Twitter) in addition to your own property?

- If you choose to participate in illegal downloading, are you mindful of the consequences of digital piracy? Are you aware of the widespread negative effects of those actions?

- When you see evidence of online abuse and bullying, how do you react? What action do you take as a digital online citizen?

Resources

A terrific resource for stopping online bullying—www.stopcyberbullying.org

A public ad campaign for the prevention of online abuse and cyberbullying—
www.ncpc.org/cyberbullying

A good web site about social responsibility online—
http://blog.safetyclicks.com/2009/06/11/parents-are-we-being-digitally-responsible

Caslon Analytics' online guide to respecting intellectual property—
www.caslon.com.au/ipguide.htm

Information Technology and Innovation Foundation's (ITIF) Strategies for Reducing Digital
Piracy—www.itif.org/index.php?id=324

Digital Citizenry Online—http://digitalcitizen.ca

Digital Citizenship Etiquette Quiz—
http://middleschooladvisory101.blogspot.com/2009/10/digital-citizenship-etiquette-
quizzes.html

Downloadable PDF on Digital Citizenship Behavior—
www.digitalcitizenship.net/uploads/1stLL.pdf

Chapter 2

Searching

> If you don't know where you're going, you'll probably end up somewhere else.
>
> **Yogi Berra**

Expectations: What Will You Learn?

In November 2006, CNN reported that the Internet had reached a milestone of 100 million web sites (Walton, 2006). This was based on research collected by Netcraft, an Internet research company. By January 2009, Netcraft estimated the Web had grown to be 185 million web sites.

In this chapter, you will use advanced search tools to harness the power of the Internet. We will use the Google™ search engine, which has become so ubiquitous that people now use the phrase "Google it" to describe searching the Internet. We will look at how to structure searches and refine them to get the maximum benefit and best information.

There are many other search engines that these principles can be applied to. These skills are transferable and applicable across these tools.

Searching Terminology

Boolean searches are searches that use the Boolean search operators AND, OR, or NOT to refine a search. For example, "dogs" AND "cats" will search for pages that contain both of the keywords "cats" and "dogs" on the same page.

Hits is the term used to describe the number of results from a search.

Keyword(s) are significant words used to describe or categorize searches or tags. For example, if you want to find a particular breed of dog, the keywords might be "dog" and "German shepherd." These keywords could then be arranged into a Boolean search for "dog" AND "German shepherd." This search will look for pages with the word "dog" and phrase "German shepherd."

PageRank is how Google ranks web pages. The higher the PageRank, the more important the page is. Pages with the highest PageRank appear first in a search.

Search engines are databases connected to the Web that allow users to locate online resources based on words and phrases entered into the search field. Examples of search engines include Google, Yahoo!, MetaCrawler, Dogpile, and so on.

URL stands for Universal Resource Locater. A URL is the web address of a page or online resource. For example *www.cnn.com* is the URL of the CNN television channel.

Web 2.0 is a term used to describe web pages and sites that allow users to add content as well as read the information provided. Web 2.0 is also called the read/write Web.

Web browsers are the software programs that allow you to surf or search the Internet. The most common web browsers are Microsoft's Internet Explorer, Mozilla's Firefox, and Apple's Safari.

What Is the Google Search Engine and "Googling"?

While there are many other search engines, Google (see Figure 2-1) has become the default tool of choice. The phrase "Google it" has now become commonly used to describe a web search. Google is a powerful search engine that allows searchers to quickly and easily find images, files, or web pages.

Figure 2-1 *Google New Zealand Search*

How Google Finds Suitable Pages

Google visits each web page and analyzes the page's content and other pages linking to that page. This is called *indexing*.

Each web page is given a rank or rating. This is called a *PageRank*. The PageRank is calculated based on the number of web pages that link to the page. A page that has 100 pages linking to it has a higher ranking than a page with 13 pages linking to it. In essence, PageRank is an Internet popularity competition with each link as a vote.

The higher the PageRank, the better or more important the page is deemed to be. The pages with the highest PageRank are the first in the search result. PageRank helps find what the search engine decides are the "best" pages for the search from the millions of pages available. Even though this is Google's interpretation of "best," it might not be the best result for you!

Using the Advanced Search

The advanced search option (see Figure 2-2) allows you to quickly refine your search using Boolean logic fields (AND, OR, NOT) and to define date ranges, file formats, language preferences, and so on. By refining the search and being specific in your requests, you should be able to quickly and simply find the specific information you need, as opposed to the information that Google *thinks* you need.

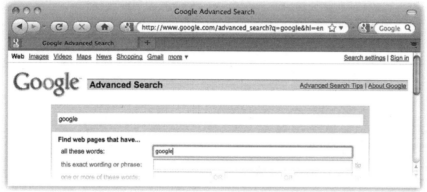

Figure 2-2 *Google Advanced Search*

How Do You Use It Personally?

Being able to easily use search engines to quickly and accurately find the information you want means that you will:

- have more time to do the things you want to do
- find the best price
- find out what is happening in your local area
- stay up-to-date with events and news
- find businesses, bargains, and friends.

Here is an example; I would like to find out about my favorite breed of dogs, the German shepherd. I am interested in buying one and would like to see what is available in my local area. I use a simple Google search (www.google.com), and I'll type in the search word "dogs" (see Figure 2-3).

Figure 2-3 *Google search for "dogs"*

The search returns 155 million pages with the term "dogs" in them. This is obviously far too many pages for me to use. Clearly, I need to refine the search. So now I put in some more specific information. I include the words "German" and "shepherd" in the search field with the word "dogs" (see Figure 2-4).

Figure 2-4 *Search for "dogs german shepherd"*

Advanced Uses

My search for "dogs" and "German" and "shepherd" has found almost 7 million pages with these three words within the page. This is still way too many pages to sort through. I click on the Advanced Search link, and this opens the Advanced Search page (see Figure 2-5).

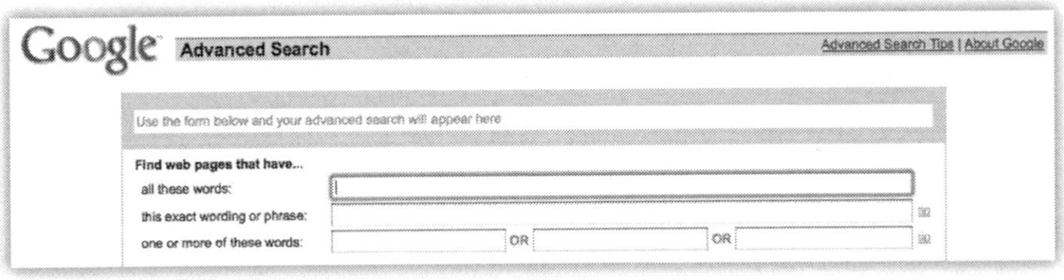

Figure 2-5 *Google advanced search*

Now I can use the Advanced Search options to refine my search (see Figure 2-6). I take the two words "German" and "shepherd" and add these to the exact wording or phrase field. This search looks for pages with the word "dogs" and the phrase "German shepherd."

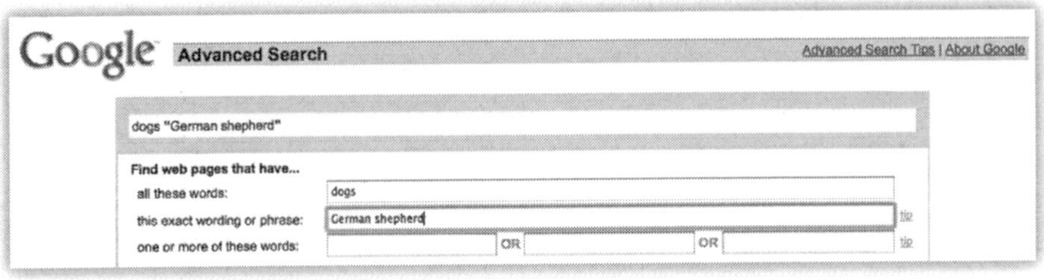

Figure 2-6 *Google advanced search*

This search helps refine my query to 2.8 million pages! This is still too many pages to be useful. Selecting the region for the search as only the United States and adding in other search terms like "breeders" and "New York" refines the search to 118,000 web pages (see Figure 2-7).

Google Advanced Search

Advanced Search Tips | About Google

dog "German shepherd"

Find web pages that have...

all these words:	dog breeders "New York"
this exact wording or phrase:	German shepherd
one or more of these words:	OR OR

Figure 2-7 *Refined search for "dog breeders"*

Keeping the same search words and phrases and setting the date range to the "past 24 hours" further refines the search to approximately 3,000 pages (see Figure 2-8).

Date, usage rights, numeric range, and more

Date: (how recent the page is)	past 24 hours
Usage rights:	not filtered by license
Where your keywords show up:	anywhere in the page
Region:	United States
Numeric range:	..
	(e.g. $1500..$3000)
SafeSearch:	⊙ Off ○ On

Advanced Search

Figure 2-8 *Google search options for "past 24 hours"*

These pages are ranked using PageRank to produce the best result (see Figure 2-9). Having refined the search, I can now contact a breeder and buy a German shepherd puppy.

The more detail you can add to the advanced search, the narrower the search becomes. Be aware that this takes a bit of practice and adjustment of your searching strategies.

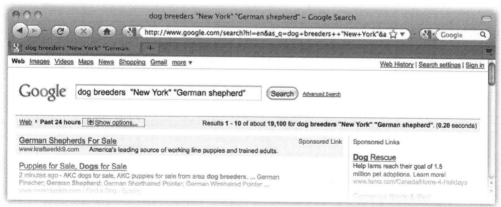

Figure 2-9 *Advanced search results*

How Do You Use It in a Classroom?

The Central African Republic of Rwanda has been ravaged by war, genocide, poverty, and disease. The students in a humanities/social studies class are researching the impact of this crisis on the people of Rwanda. The initial search using the keyword "Rwanda" produced more than 70 million pages with the word "Rwanda" in the text or images (see Figure 2-10), so the students must use advanced search options to refine the search.

Figure 2-10 *Google search for "Rwanda"*

The students add in a new key phrase in the exact wording or phrase field. The Google advanced search now looks for pages that contain the word "Rwanda" and the phrase "humanitarian crisis" (see Figure 2-11).

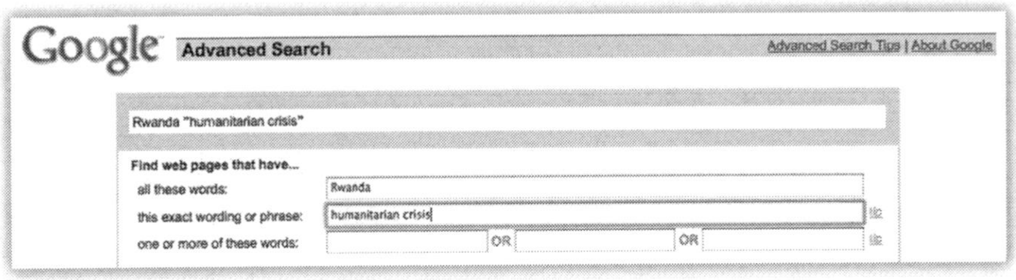

Figure 2-11 *Google advanced search for "Rwanda" and "humanitarian crisis"*

Google now treats this as a Boolean search, looking for pages that contain both the word "Rwanda" and the phrase "humanitarian crisis." Note that placing "humanitarian crisis" in quotes tells the search engine to look for that exact wording and treat the phrase as a single unit. This search results in about 118,000 hits (Figure 2-12).

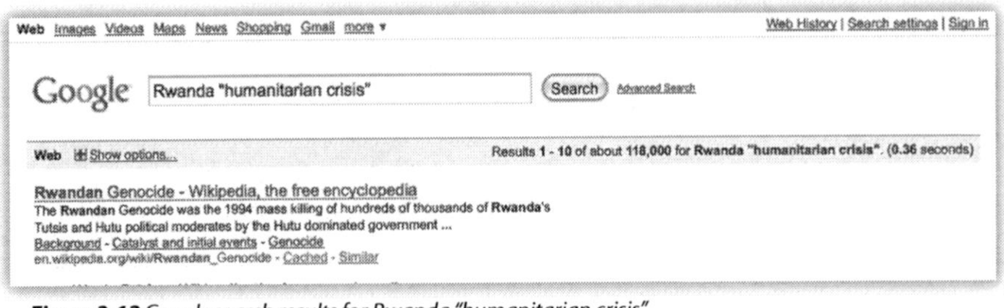

Figure 2-12 *Google search results for Rwanda "humanitarian crisis"*

These are organized using PageRank, but the criteria are still too wide to produce the detailed results the students need. The first hit in Figure 2-10 discusses the events in 1994 and does not look at current events.

The students are then briefed on how to further refine the search. They can state how recently the page was created. The students use the date option in the advanced search page (see Figure 2-13).

By setting the language option, only results in the language specified will be returned—for example, only pages written in English (see Figure 2-14).

By selecting specific web sites, the search engine will only search those sites (see Figure 2-15). For example, to only search the BBC web site, enter *bbc.co.uk* in this field.

Date: (how recent the page is)   anytime

Figure 2-13 *Date option in advanced search*

Language: any language

Figure 2-14 *Language option in advanced search*

Search within a site or domain:
(e.g. youtube.com, .edu)

Figure 2-15 *Site/Domain option in advanced search*

Specifying the keywords, limiting dates, selecting languages or domains, and so on will reduce the number of hits to manageable levels. Students who successfully refine searches are developing an understanding of not only the process of searching, but also the research topic. This search has set the date range to be within the past week while still using the keyword "Rwanda" and phrase "humanitarian crisis" (see Figure 2-16).

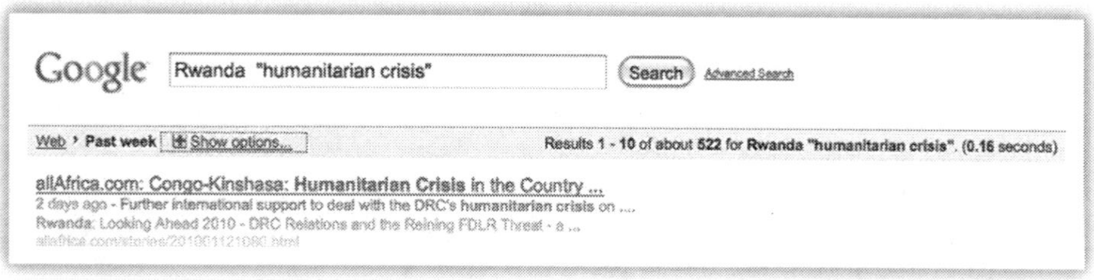

Google   Rwanda "humanitarian crisis"   Search Advanced Search

Web › Past week | Show options...   Results 1 - 10 of about 522 for Rwanda "humanitarian crisis". (0.16 seconds)

allAfrica.com: Congo-Kinshasa: Humanitarian Crisis in the Country ...
2 days ago - Further international support to deal with the DRC's humanitarian crisis on ....
Rwanda: Looking Ahead 2010 - DRC Relations and the Reining FDLR Threat - 8 ...
allafrica.com/stories/201901121080.html

Figure 2-16 *Google advanced search results*

The students are now able to access current material on the humanitarian crisis in Rwanda. They do not have to waste precious class time trying to find the most recent articles or reading pages that look at the geography or wildlife of Rwanda.

The advanced search has allowed the students to quickly access the required information with a high degree of success. They have also developed a level of understanding of the topic by structuring their searches.

✿ Classroom Examples That Cultivate The 21st Century Fluencies*

- **Solution Fluency**—Students can establish background information. Students can perform research to find suitable examples of comparable solutions or to find ideas for potential solutions. *Examples:* Research into the background of a famous figure in history; research Louis Pasteur's early life to set the scene for his discoveries in the field of medicine; research events leading to the start of World War I or the Arab-Israeli conflicts; examine the elements that resulted in the end of the Cold War.

- **Information Fluency**—Students can use Boolean and other advanced search techniques to find and organize information or validate information using other secondary information sources relating back to the original source to verify its authenticity. *Examples:* Using Boolean operators, refine searches for organizations protesting the dwindling population of marine mammals or other endangered species for an environmental project; background information on famous sea captains to determine which one the students would want to sail under; information on weather, the economy, and quality of life to determine the best place to live.

- **Collaboration Fluency**—Students can locate suitable resources and share the links for discussion through a social bookmarking tool (see Chapter 3). *Examples:* Examine current issues in climate change using advanced search techniques and social bookmarking tools to share key weather data sites; locate and share data on famous musical composers to demonstrate different musical styles.

- **Creativity Fluency**—Students can find examples of high-quality work as a source of inspiration for the design of a solution. *Examples:* Develop and use criteria to find well-designed web sites, then use those examples to design a web site; use YouTube to locate examples of well-designed video shorts and use those examples as a model for creating a video.

- **Media Fluency**—Students can locate examples of different approaches for presenting information and compare and contrast the effectiveness of those methods. *Examples:* Locate information from a variety of media sources including text-based and audiovisual media sources to provide background information for a class project; address a local issue such as traffic congestion, overcrowding, or the building of a new waterfront facility.

The 21st Century Fluencies are not about technical prowess. They are critical thinking skills, and they are essential to living in this multimedia world. An in-depth explanation of these fluencies is beyond the scope of this book. For more information, visit www.21stcenturyfluency.com

21st Century Fluency Project

Advanced Search Rubric

This is a rubric for the using advanced searches. This search requires an understanding of the keywords, Boolean logic, advanced search features, structuring and refining searches, and suitable search engines. Students need to refine the search to produce usable results and then validate these.

4 The students select a suitable search engine to use for the search and can justify their selection. They can use the advanced search page and options. The user can refine the search using most of the features of the advanced search. This may include domain, country, language, file type, or location in page. The students can justify the refinements. The students use exact match, phrase, and exclude fields; enter appropriate keyword(s); and execute the search. They modify the keywords or terms to refine the search. They can navigate through the result pages and understand the weighting system used by the specific search engine. They recognize the features of the search engine.

3 The students can select a suitable search engine to use for the search. They use the advanced search page and options. The students can refine the search using some of the features of the advanced search. This may include domain, country, language, file type, or location in page. The students can enter appropriate keyword(s) and execute the search. The students can modify the keywords or terms to refine the search. They can navigate through the result pages. They have an understanding of the weighting system used by the search engine. They can recognize features of the search engine like sponsored links.

2 The students select a search engine to use for the search. The students use the basic search page by entering appropriate keywords and speech marks for phrases. The user executes the search. The students can navigate through the result pages. The students can recognize features of the search engine like sponsored links.

1 The students select a search engine to use for the search. The students use the basic search page by entering keyword(s) and executing the search.

Summary

- Using advanced searching techniques such as the Google Advanced Search page and Boolean operators, you and your students can quickly gain access to appropriate information.

- These techniques allow you to refine searches to a manageable number of hits. The students' understanding of the topic will improve as they develop an understanding of the keywords and phrases that will help to refine their search.

- You will have more success in your searches, save time and money, and get the results you need.

Questions to Ask

- When using keyword searches, are you being specific about what you're searching for? Are your keywords giving you more index results than you need?

- How can you use keyword phrases in an advanced search to narrow your search?

- How does PageRank work, and how does it help you find online resources for your topic more efficiently?

Resources

Find out about PageRank—www.Google.com/corporate/tech.html

The essentials of Google search. This is Google's basic search hints page—
www.google.com/support/websearch/bin/static.py?page=searchguides.html&ctx=basics

Advanced searches made easy: Google's hints page on refining advanced searches—
www.google.com/support/websearch/bin/static.py?
page=searchguides.html&ctx=advanced&hl=en

Starter Sheet—Google Advanced Search: This is a starting resource for using Google advance
search—http://edorigami.wikispaces.com/Starter+Sheets

Walton Marsha. Web reaches new milestone: 100 million sites, November 1, 2006—
http://edition.cnn.com/2006/TECH/internet/11/01/100millionwebsites

Netcraft. January 2009 Web Server Survey Date, retrieved January 31, 2009—
http://news.netcraft.com/archives/2009/01/16/january_2009_web_server_survey.html

Search resources from Minich.com Internet Education—
http://minich.com/interneteducation/searching

The Spider's Apprentice Search Engine Guide—
www.monash.com/spidap.html

Anderson, L.W., & Krathwohl D. (Eds.). (2001). *A taxonomy for tearning, teaching and assessing:
A revision of Bloom's taxonomy of educational objectives*. New York: Longman.

Chapter 3
Social Bookmarking

> Imagine a world where children instantly have access to the sum total of human knowledge at their fingertips, and can move through ideas and information at the speed of thought, but where there are many teachers, parents, and citizens who cannot, and you have a metaphor for the Information Age in which we live.
>
> **Ian Jukes**

Expectations: What Will You Learn?

The Internet is too big for any of us to find all the best sites and resources to use. Enter social bookmarking, where you use the search power of all of your friends to find and save (bookmark) all the best web sites.

In this chapter, you will stretch your use of the Internet to new levels—you'll learn about finding, saving, and sharing sites with your colleagues and students, while they share theirs with you. Social bookmarking tools allow you access to your own, and your network's, bookmarks anywhere you have access to the Web.

We will explore social bookmarking using a free tool called Delicious.

Social Bookmarking Terminology

Bookmarking is a way to record a web address (URL) and title of a web page for future reference. Social bookmarking allows you to share these bookmarks with others.

Extensions are add-ons to your web browser that allow you to perform specific jobs or tasks. For example, the Delicious extension adds buttons to the browser toolbar that allow you to bookmark pages or go directly to your social bookmarking account.

Tags are keywords attached to the bookmarks. Tags are used to make searching and managing bookmarks easier.

URL stands for Universal Resource Locator. A URL is the web address of a page or online resource. For example, *www.cnn.com* is the URL of the CNN television channel.

Web browsers are the software programs that allow you to surf or search the Internet. The most common web browsers are Microsoft's Internet Explorer, Mozilla's Firefox, and Apple's Safari.

What Is Delicious?

Delicious is an online tool that allows users to save web addresses or URLs to their personal accounts (see Figure 3-1). The service is free and simply requires users to register.

Adding extensions to your browsers (Firefox and Internet Explorer) adds buttons to the toolbars that allow you to quickly bookmark web sites. You can then organize the bookmarks, adding tags and notes, which makes them easy to sort into topics and searches, as well as share with your network.

Since URLs can be saved in a portable format, they can be reached from any computer attached to the Internet by any browser.

Figure 3-1 *www.delicious.com*

Why Did We Select Delicious?

Delicious is a powerful social networking tool that is widely used. There are extensions available for most of the common browsers that enable seamless recording and sharing of bookmarks. Delicious is not the only social bookmarking tool in town. Another example is Diigo (www.diigo.com).

Why Do You Use Social Bookmarking?

If you save your favorite web sites using Favorites in Microsoft's Internet Explorer or Bookmarks in Mozilla's Firefox, these sites are recorded only on the computer you used to save them. Without some sort of system of management, web sites are not easily searched or sorted; they are hard to manage and almost impossible to share.

Social bookmarking tools overcome these problems. The bookmarks are saved in an account accessible from any computer (see Figure 3-2). The bookmarks can be categorized by using keywords called tags. These tags are searchable. As you browse the Web, you will invariably find interesting sites that you might want to refer to in the future.

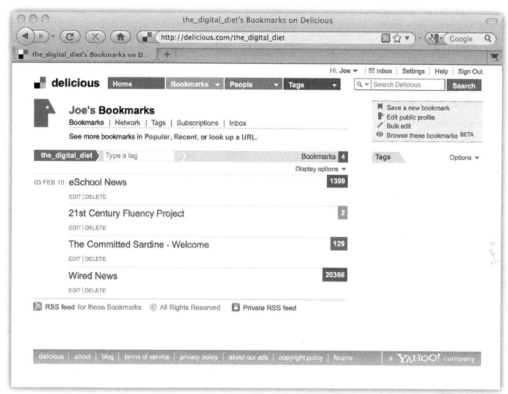

Figure 3-2 *A typical Delicious bookmark list*

By bookmarking these sites now, in the future you can search for the best sites in your bookmarks by selecting the keywords, and others in your network can share theirs with you (see Figure 3-3). Or you can keep your bookmarks private if you wish. Social bookmarks are searchable, manageable, accessible, and collaborative. They are an ideal tool for adults and children alike.

Figure 3-3 *Navigating Delicious via the navigation buttons. The buttons are links to your home, bookmarks, tags, network, inbox, and subscriptions.*

How Do You Use Social Bookmarking Personally?

Using a social bookmarking tool is quite straightforward. The tool being used for this example is Delicious, but there are many other social bookmarking tools available.

First, you need to create an account (free). Go to the Delicious web site at http://del.icio.us or www.delicious.com and click on Join Now. You will be asked to enter some basic details and an account will be created (see Figure 3-4).

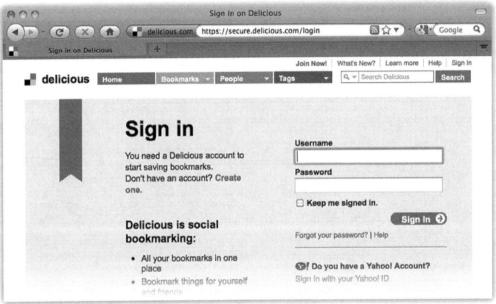

Figure 3-4 *Delicious getting started page*

You can install browser extensions to add buttons to your toolbar if you wish. Most of the common web browsers have extensions or plug-ins that add Delicious buttons to the browser's toolbar. These buttons allow one-click bookmarking (recording of web sites) by opening your Delicious account (see Figure 3-5).

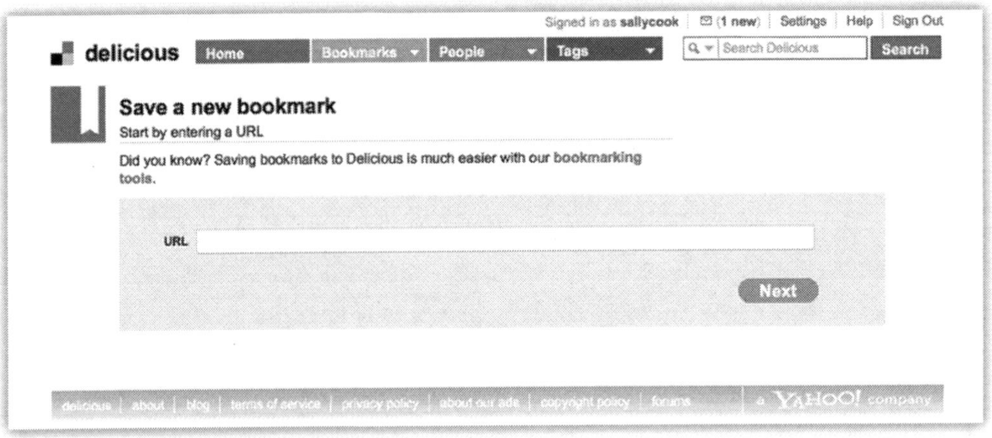

Figure 3-5 *Delicious "save bookmark"*

When you click on the Delicious button on your toolbar, a separate window opens with spaces to add key information, such as tags, notes, and so on. You can then share the bookmark with your network (see Figure 3-6).

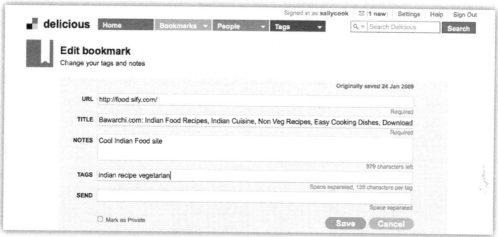

Figure 3-6 *Delicious "edit bookmark"*

Delicious Bookmarks Make Saving Recipes a Snap

Sally is an enthusiastic cook who has often used the Internet to find interesting recipes to share with her friends. She does this by copying the web address of the site and emailing it to them. Often, her friends will ask her several times for the same web site or the same recipe. Sally has saved all of these sites to her Favorites in her web browser, which means that she has to be at home and working on her computer to share them with her friends.

Sally opens a social bookmarking account on Delicious. She transfers all her saved bookmarks from her computer (Delicious allows you to import these directly to your account). She then sorts them into categories using tags, or keywords (starters, main dishes, and desserts), and themes (Indian, Mexican, French, Chinese, traditional, and so on). She encourages her friends to start their own Delicious accounts and then adds them to her network. They can now share their latest discoveries and have access to Sally's best recipe sites, which they can save to their own bookmarks. Now they can all easily search for recipes using the tags (keywords) and share those recipes with others.

Advanced Uses

Delicious is not just limited to saving and sharing bookmarks. There is a lot more you can try and do. Here are ideas to explore:

- Some bookmarks can be marked as private and are only available for you to see. Try the "Mark as private" option when you tag a page.

- Try subscriptions. A subscription is a way to collect the recent bookmarks that everybody has saved with the tags or keywords you are interested in. Once you start a subscription, the tags will appear on your subscription page.

- Bundle your network. Network bundles are a way of grouping people in your network into manageable sets. Go to your network page and click on the "manage your network" option on the right-hand pane.

- Post your tags to your blog. Delicious has a powerful tool that allows you to update your blog and automatically post your tags and notes.

How Do You Use It in a Classroom?

Social bookmarking tools like Delicious are brilliant tools not only for remembering URLs or web locations, but also for collaboration. Delicious users share bookmarks with other members of their network. It's easy to add people to your network. Simply click on the network icon on the Delicious page and add the person's Delicious name. Then when you find a site, distribute it to the appropriate members of your network.

Students and staff alike should use the keywords and notes to make retrieval of saved locations easier. The more detailed and accurate the keywords, the easier it is to organize and search for resources. If students are working together on a class project, they could all be required to contribute information they have researched and the sources they have identified. To facilitate this, the teacher and the students can create class and personal Delicious accounts, and then share these accounts with one another.

Now when the students (or teachers) are bookmarking sites, they add the tags field to the class account. They also add appropriate keywords and notes to their bookmarks. When they tag a site to the class account (or a member of their network), the new bookmark appears in their inbox, waiting for the teacher to moderate the site as suitable and either save the tag or delete it.

The teacher moderates the URLs submitted by the students by either saving or deleting the bookmarks. The teacher can also see the level of understanding in the students' selection from the notes and tags. The students and teachers can now share and collaborate on their research and learning.

Classroom Examples That Cultivate The 21st Century Fluencies

- **Solution Fluency**—Students can locate, record, annotate, and share suitable information sources and examples of suitable tools for development of a solution. *Example:* Build a list of green energy sources to power a laptop while camping; find a list of resources for printing custom coffee mugs to sell as a fundraiser for purchasing equipment.

- **Information Fluency**—Students can locate, process, collate, and share information sources for analysis and use keywords and notes to efficiently retrieve information. *Examples:* Share web-based resources related to the Olympics, the World Cup, a golf tournament, or sports playoffs as part of learning within a unit focused on sporting events.

- **Collaboration Fluency**—Students can share and use key resources with peers (i.e., metatags, keywords, summaries) to distribute the workload and increase the quality of a finished product. *Examples:* Research various historical figures such as Euclid, Descartes, Gauss, and Escher to develop an understanding of the historical context of geometric theory.

- **Creativity Fluency**—Students can record exemplars of good and bad solutions and share them with colleagues; tools and processes that may stimulate and refine the development of creative products; examples of different mind mapping techniques that are used to structure and analyze information like the fishbone, tree charts, spreadsheets, and Venn diagrams.

- **Media Fluency**—Students can locate, record, and critique exemplars of multiple approaches and styles to presentation of information. *Example:* Investigate, locate, and share different genres of films as part of a comparative study of television and film from available sources like YouTube and Vimeo.

21st Century Fluency Project

Social Bookmarking Rubric

This is a sample rubric for bookmarking. The rubric covers bookmarking or saving favorites using an Internet browser and social bookmarking tools.

4 The user adds URLs to a social bookmarking site. The user adds detailed comments or appropriate keywords or tags. The comments essentially summarize the resource and are appropriate and useful. There is little duplication of tags. The web sites are bookmarked on the basis of validity (validates). The user shares the bookmark with appropriate members of his or her network.

3 The user adds URLs to a social bookmarking site and adds comments or tags. Tags are mostly well-constructed and suitable keywords. There is some duplication of tags (such as singular and plural keywords). There is some limited filtering on the basis of validity (attempts validation). The comments or notes are simple. The user shares the bookmark with all members of his or her network.

2 The user adds sites to Favorites (Internet Explorer) or Bookmarks (Firefox). The bookmarks are organized into folders, which are appropriately named. Or, the user adds URLs to a social bookmarking site. The user sometimes adds either tags (keywords) or comments/notes. The resources are added regardless of their value or validity.

1 The user adds sites to Favorites (Internet Explorer), Bookmarks (Firefox), or a social bookmarking site. The user does not add tags or comments. The locally stored bookmarks lack structure or organization.

Summary

- Using social bookmarking tools, students and teachers are able to harness the huge potential of the Internet's resources by collaborating and sharing sites they have found and validated.

- The easy accessibility of social bookmarking tools means you can access and search your bookmarks from any computer connected to the Internet.

- Students are easily able to collaborate with their peers and teachers, which contributes to the learning process and validates their research process.

Questions to Ask

- How does using a social bookmarking site like Delicious differ from simply saving site bookmarks in "Favorites"?

- What is a tag, and how is it used in efficient social bookmarking?

- How can subscriptions add to your list of page resources in a bookmarking site?

- How can a social bookmarking site help with sharing resources between students and teachers in the classroom environment?

Resources

Social Bookmarking in Plain English: This excellent video from the Commoncraft show explains the process and benefits of social bookmarking in three minutes— www.commoncraft.com/bookmarking-plain-english

Delicious help: The Delicious help pages are well laid out and simple to use. These pages answer all of the FAQs (Frequently Asked Questions) and much more— http://Del.icio.us .com/help/learn

Educause: Seven things you should know about Social Bookmarking. This is an excellent resource in the monthly series of learning resources produced by Educause. This publication looks at the educational use of social bookmarking— http://connect.educause.edu/Library/ELI/7ThingsYouShouldKnowAbout/39378

Underground Training Lab Social Bookmarking Tutorial—www.undergroundtraininglab.com/ 25/social-bookmarking-tutorial

Slideshare Delicious tutorial—www.slideshare.net/maggiev/delicious-tutorial-presentation

Social bookmarking basics on YouTube—www.youtube.com/watch?v=meyiH9E60hY

The Tlog Delicious tutorial—http://sites.dehumanizer.com/delicious/en/delicious.php

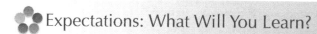

Chapter 4
Collaborative Editing

> How can you be in two places at once,
> when you're not anywhere at all?
>
> **Groucho Marx**

Expectations: What Will You Learn?

In previous chapters of this book, you searched for information using the Google Advanced Search, and then used the social bookmarking tool Delicious to save those sites and share the information with your network.

In this chapter, you will collaboratively build documents and share them using Adobe's Buzzword. Buzzword is an online word processor with a fun, simple interface. There are lots of word processors available, but Buzzword has the ability to foster collaboration by allowing users to share the same document. Buzzword is only one of a number of online productivity tools.

Collaborative Editing Terminology

File format describes the way information in a document is organized and saved. Usually each productivity tool saves documents that are created in its own file format. For example, Microsoft Word will save in the .doc format developed by Microsoft. OpenOffice Writer will save files in the Open Document Format, or .odf. This can sometimes cause issues of compatibility between files created by different productivity tools.

Online means that the application or tool must be accessed through the Internet. Some online tools also have the ability to be used offline.

Online collaborative editing uses an online word-processing resource to allow more than one person to edit and work on a document.

Presentation tools are tools that allow users to enter information such as text, images, video, and sound, and then present it in a suitable format, usually slideshow style. Examples of presentation tools include StarOffice and OpenOffice Impress, Apple's iWork Keynote, and Microsoft PowerPoint.

Productivity tools is the term used to describe work-related tools like word processors, spreadsheets, presentation tools, and so on. Offline examples of productivity suites include software such as Microsoft Office, Sun's StarOffice, and the open source OpenOffice 3.0. There are also online productivity suites, such as Google Documents and Zoho Documents.

Spreadsheets are tools that allow users to enter, format, and process data using columns, rows, formulas, and equations. Examples of spreadsheets include software such as Microsoft Excel, StarOffice Calc, OpenOffice Calc, and Apple's Numbers.

Word processors are tools that allow users to enter and format text into documents. Some examples are Microsoft Word, StarOffice Writer, OpenOffice Writer, and Apple's Pages.

What Are Buzzword and Online Collaborative Editing?

Buzzword is an Internet-based word processor that allows users to either create a document or import a document from a variety of file formats, and then collaboratively edit and format that same document. Once completed, users can export the document in a wide variety of file formats. Like all word processors, Buzzword allows you to enter and format text, store and retrieve files, and print to attached printers. Buzzword is a free service provided by Adobe.

Why Did We Select Buzzword?

Sometimes it's hard to look beyond Google and select other products, but in this case we decide to step past Google Docs and look at Adobe's Buzzword. Buzzword gives us a clean and simple word processor that we can access from anywhere at anytime. Buzzword has similarities to both Google Documents and Zoho Documents and, as a result, the skills you develop in one product are transferable to other online and offline tools, such as Microsoft Word or Apple's Pages.

Here are two other options to try:

- Google Documents (spreadsheet, word processor, presentation tool, and more)—http://doc.google.com.
- Zoho suite of tools (spreadsheet, word processor, presentation tool, and more)—www.zoho.com.

Buzzword is part of Acrobat.com and it's not just a word processor, it is also a presentation tool and a spreadsheet. To use Buzzword, you first have to register and create an Adobe ID (see Figure 4-1). This is your online profile. Your Adobe ID will require the following:

- your email address so you can be invited to collaborate on documents
- your first and last name for tracking changes and edits
- a password to secure the documents from unauthorized editing
- your country and language information

Once the profile is completed, you are ready to start.

Join Adobe

Adobe Membership is free and registration only takes a minute. As a member, you will have access to trial downloads, hundreds of free product extensions, and special community areas. Your membership also allows you to view and manage your activity in the Adobe Worldwide Store.

* Required fields

Your privacy is important to us. Please read our privacy policy.

ACCOUNT DETAILS

E-mail *	
Password * (Must be between 6-12 characters)	
Retype password *	
Password hint	
First name *	
Last name *	
Job title	SELECT
Organization name	
Address	
City *	
Country/Region *	Canada

Figure 4-1 *Adobe sign up*

Buzzword starts with the Document Organizer (see Figure 4-2). The Document Organizer allows you to access old documents and start new ones. You can also invite others to share or collaborate and organize meetings to work or comment on documents.

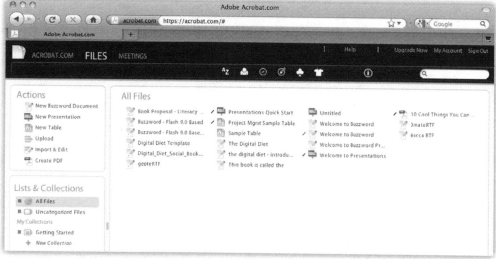

Figure 4-2 *Buzzword Document Organizer*

The Sort Options allow you to arrange the documents in the Document Organizer. The Document menu (see Figure 4-3) allows you to manage the documents, including:

- importing documents in a variety of formats, including Microsoft Word (.xml, .doc, .docx), plain text (.txt), Rich Text Format (.rtf), and Open Document Format (.odt)

- exporting documents in a variety of formats, including portable document format (.pdf), Microsoft Word (.doc, .docx), plain text (.txt), Rich Text Format (.rtf), and Open Document Format (.odt)

- deleting existing documents

Figure 4-3 Document menu

What's With the File Formats?

Different software tools, like Apple's iWork or Microsoft Office, save their files in different formats, and different versions of the software can also save in different formats. There isn't a universal file format that allows us to exchange files between all software tools.

Many of the software tools we use will open files from many different formats, but sometimes they change in the translation. This can cause problems if we are not careful. A table you have placed in one spot in a document can suddenly appear in a different position if you open the document in a different program.

Some programs will not be able to open some file formats. Microsoft's latest version of Office—Office 2007—creates documents in a new format called .docx. Many of the older word processors are not able to open these files.

Step 1: Start a New Document

You can start a new document by using the Document menu and selecting New or clicking on the New Document icon on the toolbar. This will create a new blank document (see Figure 4-4).

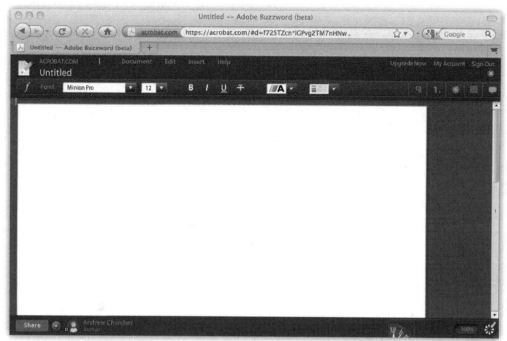

Figure 4-4 *New blank document*

Step 2: Enter and Format Text

At this point, Buzzword looks like any other word processor. Type in the text, and then if you want to change how the text, a table, or a list appears, you simply place your mouse on the character, word, paragraph, or object you want to format. Next, you click on the menu to get access to the range of tools (see Figure 4-5). The Buzzword menus expand and contract to reveal and hide formatting tools and options. The various Buzzword menus are accessed using the menu icons on the tool bar (see Figure 4-6).

Figure 4-5 *New document toolbar*

Figure 4-6 *Toolbar expanded for "fonts"*

What Tools Do I Have?

Because Buzzword is a simple word processor, it contains the basic tools set (Figures 4-5, 4-6 on the previous page). Some of these tools include:

- *Font format*—selects font type (such as Arial, Times New Roman, and so on), font weight (normal or bold), font size (10 pt, 12 pt, and so on), font style (normal, italics, boldface, and so on) and font colors

- *Lists*—to add bullet points or numbers to a list

- *Paragraph*—starts a new paragraph

- *Tables*—allows you to insert a custom table graphic

- *Symbols*—add and edit graphics or pictures within the document tables, insert and modify

- *Comments*—allows authors, coauthors, and reviewers to enter comments in the documents that can be viewed by other collaborators but do not change the form of the original document

Step 3: Let's Share!

You can invite your colleagues and students to collaborate on a document by clicking on the Share button. Then enter the person's email address (or select them from a list) and set their role as a coauthor, reviewer, or reader (see Figure 4-7).

Once the document has been shared, other coauthors can edit it; however, it's important to note that only one person can edit a document at a time.

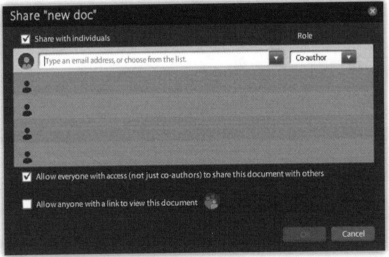

Figure 4-7 *Document share window*

The Status bar at the bottom of the document shows the different roles each person has. A person who is editing a document will have editing in red by his or her name on the status bar, a person viewing a document will have viewing in yellow beside his or her name.

The person who started the document is the author. Coauthors have full editing rights, while reviewers can read the document and make comments but cannot change the content of the document.

How Do You Use Buzzword Personally?

Buzzword and other similar tools, like Google Documents and Zoho Documents, are powerful enablers of collaboration. The following is an example concerning this very book itself.

This book was written between several principal authors, Ian and Lee in Canada and Andrew in New Zealand. If we used a traditional word processing or document creation process, this is what would have occurred:

- Andrew would write the document and then fax or email it to Ian and Lee in Canada for their contribution, feedback, and review.

- They would then return the document by either fax or email.

- Andrew would then either edit the corrections and additions that Lee and Ian had made or ignore them completely and then send the document back to Ian and Lee to be rechecked.

The process would make collaborating across 12,000 miles and several hours of time difference difficult, if not impossible.

By using Buzzword to collaborate on chapters and teleconferencing using Skype (more on this in Chapter 5) to have regular face-to-face meetings, we were able to craft this book. Documents are created in a shared environment where all members of the team can see the work in progress and contribute.

The History feature allows everyone to track the changes (see Figure 4-8). The Comments tool allows reviewers to post suggestions and recommendations. Whether it's a newsletter for a club or organization, a training diary for a half marathon, a shopping list for a family holiday, or a letter written by the family to include in Christmas cards, collaborative editing using tools like Buzzword makes contributing and sharing simple and straightforward.

Figure 4-8 Documents History feature

Advanced Uses

Following are some interesting tools and techniques you can use to extend and enhance your use of Buzzword:

- Create a meeting—This feature allows you to schedule a meeting and invite participants using Adobe's ConnectNow. This tool supports video and audioconferencing, has a whiteboard pod, chat space, and shared screens. It takes collaboration on a shared document one step further, as you can host a meeting and invite participants to work with you.

- Create a spreadsheet in Table and integrate it into your Buzzword document. Table is Buzzword's spreadsheet tool.

- Work simultaneously with other users in Table. Use Private view so you do not disturb other collaborators as you make changes.

- Use the Comments feature to draft and provide formative assessment on students' work.

How Do You Use It in a Classroom?

Erin is an English teacher who has a class of 10-year-old students engaged in a novel study. The students have a range of reading ability levels. Erin's differentiated teaching program means that students are reading a selection of novels suited to their reading ability, rather than selecting one novel and trying to fit it across the ability levels.

Since the students are working in small groups, Erin decides they should collaboratively develop a book report for their novel. However, she is concerned that some students may not contribute equitably to the task and needs a tool that will show her the individual contributions of the group and allow her to monitor the group's progress. Erin understands that one of the most important techniques she has for enhancing the students' learning is timely and appropriate feedback. Ideally her tool should also enable feedback.

Erin uses Buzzword as her tool of choice for this task. She has written a template for her students and structured the document with headings and explanations. She saves multiple copies of the template by using Save As, and identifies each document with the name of the novel.

She has each student create an account on Buzzword, and adjusts each document to suit the novel and the student's ability. She then shares the document with her students by inviting them individually to collaborate using the share feature of Buzzword.

The History feature of Buzzword allows her to monitor the students' engagement in the task and to check their progress. She adds comments about the students' work, providing them with timely and appropriate feedback using the Comments feature. Each student's work is individually colored to allow Erin to measure involvement and the student's contribution. Once a consensus has been reached about the completion of the task, the students email a copy of their collaboratively developed assignment to Erin.

Classroom Examples That Cultivate The 21st Century Fluencies

- **Solution Fluency**—Students can share a single document to develop multiple approaches to solutions. *Example:* Create and publish a student newspaper by working collaboratively to develop and edit copy online prior to printing and distribution.

- **Information Fluency**—Students can obtain a broad range of perspectives and commentaries from multiple information sources and a variety of individual experiences. *Example:* Collaborate on a film review, providing a joint commentary and synopsis of the film from each student's different perspective and experience.

- **Collaboration Fluency**—Students can establish and demonstrate appropriate processes and guidelines for collaboratively developing a solution. *Examples:* Collaboratively develop and moderate learning resources and curriculum content as part of the educational process within an Information Technology class; research and report on the strengths and weaknesses of various data storage devices such as hard drives, pen drives, optical discs, and cloud computing.

- **Creativity Fluency**—Students can explore multiple perspectives and experiences, as well as the work of others, to gain inspiration for a collaborative solution. They will merge ideas to take designs to the next level. *Examples:* Brainstorm ideas and concepts in a shared environment before deciding on a solution that will be the focus of a group presentation; identify presentation methods that could be used in a performance and determine how each could be used to present the same message.

- **Media Fluency**—Students can draw on the experience base of the peers to develop a variety of media approaches to a solution and collaboratively compare the effectiveness of each. *Examples:* Determine which media approach to use for presenting a report on a favorite poem by Robert Burns or William Wordsworth. Compare the advantages and disadvantages of using blogs, wikis, podcasts, vodcasts, video, animation, and VoiceThreads for the presentation.

Summary

- Adobe Buzzword is more than just a word processor; it is part of a powerful suite of tools that can enhance your personal and professional learning, while enabling collaboration and cooperation.

- The shared document feature is useful in the classroom and in our personal lives. The anywhere, anytime access means learning is not restricted to the classroom or computer suite, nor is it limited by file compatibility or software version. Internet access means we can be in touch—sharing, working, and learning anywhere we have a computer.

- We can extend our use of Buzzword by using Meetings. We can set up meetings and arrange multiperson video and audioconferencing with this useful tool.

Questions to Ask

- What is an online word processor, and why is it good for collaborative work on a writing project?

- What do we have to be aware of in regard to file formats and how files can be interpreted from one word processor to another?

- How can a teacher use Buzzword to monitor and guide collaborative effort between groups in school writing projects?

- How can you avoid interfering with other collaborators on your project as you each work simultaneously in Buzzword?

Resources

What can you do with Adobe Buzzword? This is a document from Adobe about Buzzword and
its features—http://help.adobe.com/en_US/Acrobat.com/Buzzword/

Buzzwords tips: This is a starting page for hints, tips, and how-tos for Adobe Buzzword—
http://help.adobe.com/en_US/Acrobat.com/Buzzword/
WS623D15BC-17E5-4965-839C-3EF20098FDAA.html

Google Docs Help: This is the starter page for the three Google tools: Documents,
Presentations, and Spreadsheets—http://documents.google.com/support/?hl=en-GB

Buzzword Help Document: This is a downloadable resource for Buzzword from the Adobe
web site—http://help.adobe.com/en_US/Acrobat.com/Buzzword/buzzword_help.pdf

Starter Sheet: Buzzword: This is a two-page resource for using Buzzword in a classroom
situation—http://edorigami.wikispaces.com/Starter+Sheets

14 Interesting Ways to Use Google Docs in the Classroom: A Google documents presentation
on classroom use of Google documents by Tom Barrett—
http://docs.google.com/Present?docid=dhn2vcv5_8323t58h3ft

Chapter 5
VoIP

In hunting culture, kids play with bows and arrows. In an information society, they play with information.

Henry Jenkins

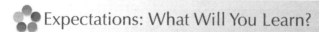

Expectations: What Will You Learn?

In this chapter, you will explore the huge range of opportunities provided to you by use of the Internet-based telephone and videoconferencing tool Skype.

You will set up a free account and learn how to chat, talk, and videoconference with your friends and colleagues. You will uncover the multiperson audioconferencing feature and use Skype to exchange documents, photos, and other files.

This part of your digital diet will have you communicating with your friends and colleagues anywhere in the world for free.

VoIP Terminology

Alphanumeric is a password that contains numbers and letters.

Broadband or **high-speed** is a fast Internet connection. Having a fast rate of information transfer is good for audio and videoconferencing. As a general rule, the faster your connection is, the better the quality of the sound or picture you send or receive will be.

Chat is a method of transferring written or typed messages between computers. In Skype, the chat window allows you to transfer files as well.

Client is the software that allows you to connect to the Skype server and communicate with other people who are online at the same time. You will have to download and install the Skype client to be able to use this tool.

Dial-up is a slow-speed connection to the Internet using a modem attached to a phone line. The transfer rate of information is very low, so dial-up is unsuitable for audio or video conferencing.

Firewall is a piece of software (or a physical device or machine in organizations) that controls connections into and out of your computer. Firewalls are an essential tool for keeping your computer and your data safe.

Offline is when your Internet connection is inactive or switched off.

Online means having an active and functional Internet connection.

Server is the central computer (actually, it's quite a few computers) that manages and routes your Skype calls.

VoIP stands for Video or Voice over Internet Protocol. Essentially, this is a set of rules that allows you to use your computer and an Internet connection to communicate with people who also have the VoIP client software active on their computer.

Why Did We Select Skype?

Skype is a well-established and widely used service. It is cross-platform, so it is available on Windows, Linux, and Mac computers. Skype's basic service is free and allows multiperson voice conferencing, as well as one-to-one videoconferencing. There are other services emerging into the VoIP area. Google has two offerings. The first is video and voice chat using its Gmail chat and the second is in the Google Wave environment, which supports extensions including multiperson videoconferencing.

What Is Skype?

Skype and other VoIP services allow you to use a computer and broadband Internet connection like a telephone or videophone. Just like a telephone system, you can:

- set up a voice mail (this is a paid service, not a free one)
- phone people, talk to people, or leave messages (if their Skype account has voicemail)
- build a list of frequently used numbers
- search a directory for people's Skype name (these are the equivalent of phone numbers)
- phone landlines (for conventional phone lines; this too is a paid service, not a free one).

But unlike telephone, Skype has a number of other features, including:

- seeing who is online and available to talk and who is away
- managing who has the ability to contact you by allowing and blocking calls
- seeing basic information and contact details of your contacts
- videoconferencing, if your computer has a video or web camera
- chat using written text
- transfer of files
- multiperson voice conference calls

To use Skype you need four things:

- *A microphone and speakers*—This could be a microphone and earphones set, or it could be speakers and a microphone built into your computer. An inexpensive web camera (again, either built in or added on to your computer) will allow you to videoconference.

- *A broadband Internet connection*—You need broadband (fast Internet) because you are transferring large amounts of information when you are using video or audio chats.

- *A Skype account*—This is a free account that you set up by going to www.skype.com. We will go through how to set up an account later in this chapter.

- *The Skype client*—You need to download the Skype software from the Skype web site and install it on you computer (see Figure 5-1). There are different versions of the software based on your computer's operating system.

Once you have set up your computer and installed the software, you can connect to the Skype services and communicate with any of your friends who are online and available.

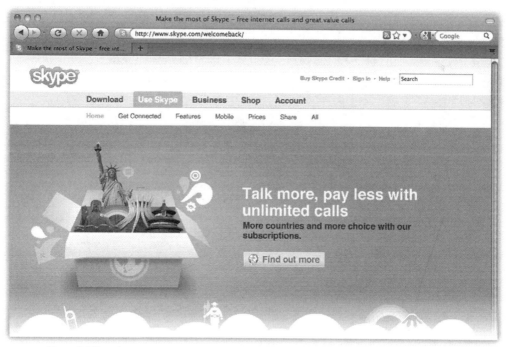

Figure 5-1 *Skype home page*

How Do You Use It Personally?

They say talk is cheap, but with Skype, talk, video, and chat are free. If you are a Skype user, you can talk or videoconference with your friends around the world for free. Whether you use it for keeping in touch with family as they travel, having conversations with friends, organizing business deals, family voice conferences, or even professional learning, Skype is a simple-to-use, everyday tool that enhances communication and saves you money.

It has been said that 90 percent of communication is nonverbal. When a person speaks to us face to face, we read a huge amount from their body language and facial expressions.

A telephone removes this key information source from us, but with a video call we regain this enormous aspect of our communication.

Let's walk through the process of setting up your Skype account and learn about using this great communication tool. The first stage of the process is to sign up for Skype to get your account and download and install the Skype software.

Go to the Skype web site at www.skype.com. Click on the Download Skype button (see Figure 5-2).

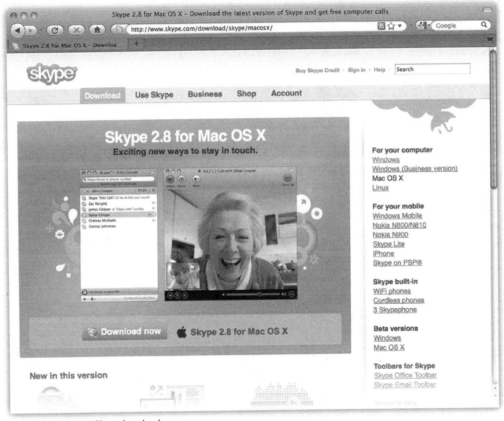

Figure 5-2 *Skype download page*

This brings you to the download page. The page will ask you to download and run a small file that will manage the installation process for setting up Skype on your computer (see Figure 5-3).

Once the Skype software has been downloaded, you will then need to run the software in order to install Skype on your computer.

Make sure you select the correct language for you, and it is always a good idea to read the license agreement.

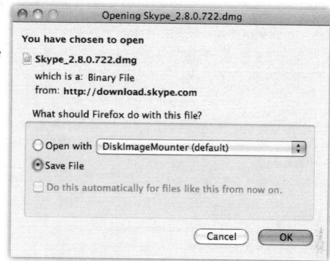

Figure 5-3 Skype run-file

When you are ready, click on the "I agree and install" button, and Skype will then begin the download process (see Figure 5-4).

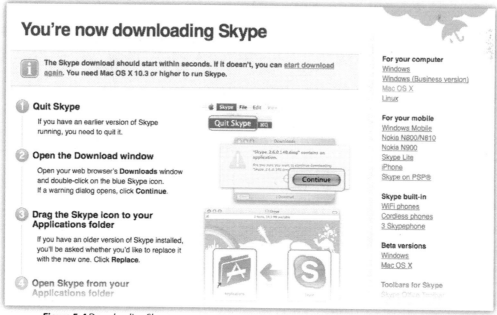

Figure 5-4 Downloading Skype

The Skype installer then downloads the software and sets it up on your computer. As it installs, you will be asked whether you want Skype to start up and log in as soon as you turn on your computer (see Figure 5-5).

If you have not set up an account, you need to click on the "Don't have a Skype name?" link, which will take you through setting up your account (see Figure 5-6). You will be asked to provide some basic details when you set up a Skype name. These include:

- *Your full name*—This is optional.

- *Your Skype name*—This is the name that your friends and other people will see when you are online and in the Skype directory. It is important that this name is appropriate and suitable. Having an obscure name will make it hard, if not impossible, for others to find you on Skype (see Chapter 1).

- *Your password*—Your password needs to be at least six characters long and be alphanumeric (contains at least one number and one letter).

- *Your email address.*

- *Your country and city.*

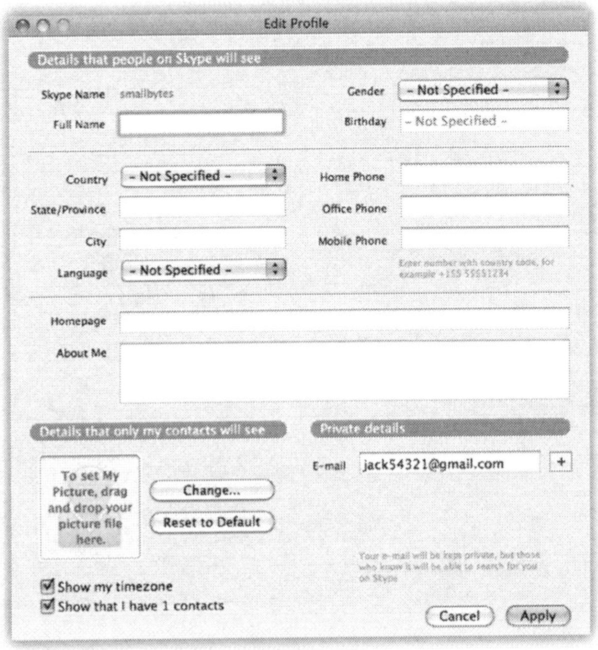

Figure 5-5 *Skype sign in*

Figure 5-6 *Skype account setup*

This completes the setup process. You can now start to Skype your friends. Skype provides a tutorial that you can use to look at the features and how to use them. This is a great starting place for new users.

One of the first steps most people take is to personalize their Skype. This can include adding pictures, details of contact information, and so on. You can also set your privacy settings.

The Skype Test Call service is the first call most people make. You call an answering service that will check to make sure your speakers and microphone are working. To call this service, just click on the Echo/Sound Test Service address in the Contacts list and then click on the Call button (see Figure 5-7 at right).

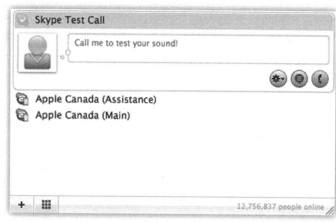

Figure 5-7 Skype test call

To adjust your audio settings, click on the Call menu and select Audio Settings (see figure 5-8). This allows you to select and adjust the microphone, speakers, and ring tone.

Figure 5-8 Skype audio settings

The Navigation pane on the left-hand side of the window allows you to adjust the other settings, including privacy notifications, calls, instant messaging, and chat.

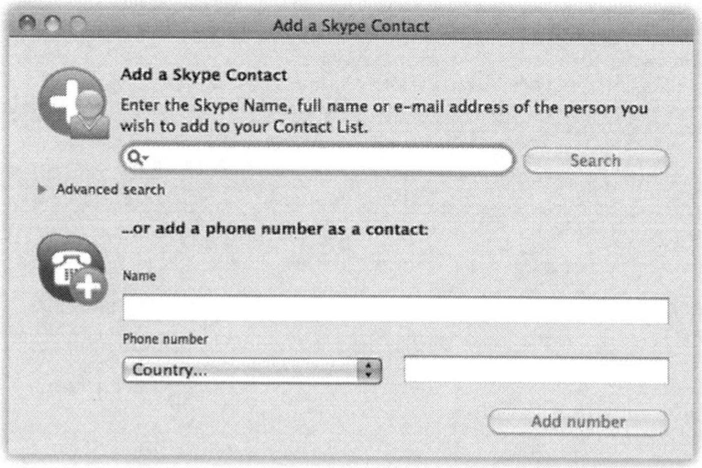

Now let's find some friends to talk to. To do this, click on the New button. This gives you these two options: New Contact or New Group Conversation. Select New Contact, which opens a new window (see Figure 5-9). Enter the person's Skype name, full name, or email address.

Figure 5-9 Add new contact

Skype then searches through the directory for people who match these details. Click on the person's details and then click on Add Contact to include them in your contacts list.

Are You Here or Not? (Status)

One of the cool features of Skype is setting your Status (see Figure 5-10). There are several different settings you can select to show your online status. The status you set is what is seen by your contacts.

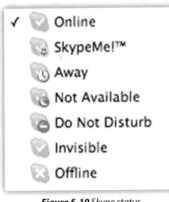

Figure 5-10 Skype status

Your list of status options includes:

- *Online*—This is the status for online and available to chat, talk, or video.

- *Away*—This means you are online but not at your computer.

- *Do Not Disturb*—This will stop people from being able to call you and is useful if you are on an important call and do not want to receive other calls.

- *Invisible*—With this selection you are online, but showing up as if you are offline.

- *Offline*—You are offline and unavailable to chat, talk, or video.

Making a Call Using Video

Select the person you would like to call and if video is available, you will have two call buttons available to you: Call and Video Call (see Figure 5-11).

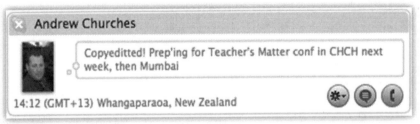

Figure 5-11 Call or video call

Figure 5-12 on the next page shows a video conversation. The call out shows the options you can use in the chat pane. You can add emoticons or send files, and the extras option allows you to play games or use add-ons like call recorders.

To add more people to your conversation, you need to stop your video, by clicking on the stop video button, and select Add People. You can add people from your contact list or by adding their landline phone number.

Figure 5-12 *Skype video call*

Advanced Uses

Once you have mastered the basics, there are some tricks and techniques you may want to try:

- Set up groups of callers for regular conference calls.
- Add extensions such as Pamela Call Recorder or the Whiteboard to your Skype service to facilitate learning.
- Use Skype to connect to landlines and mobile phones.
- Use Skype and videoconferencing as part of your personal learning network (PLN).

How Do I Use It in a Classroom?

There are many uses for video and audioconferencing in the classroom. Attaching a laptop to a projector and speakers and arranging a guest speaker is one technique that is frequently used. For guest speaker sessions to be effective, we need to look at having them properly structured. The simple 5P Rule applies here:

The 5P Rule

Proper **P**lanning **P**revents **P**oor **P**erformance

The most successful sessions I have run have been sessions that are well prepared in advance. Here are some suggestions.

- Carefully select the guest speaker. Let him or her know the purpose of the session and who the target audience is.
- Clearly define the topic.
- Have the students research the topic and develop questions.
- Combine all the questions and have the students process and validate them.
- Send the question list to the guest speaker in advance.
- Assign questions to students and have the students rehearse introducing themselves and asking the questions (very useful for younger students).
- Do a technical test beforehand, preferably at the same time you would be having your session (this will hopefully mimic the load on the network).

Have the students consider the following:

- Are the questions open or closed?
- Are the questions focused and related to the topic?
- Are the questions clear and easy to understand?
- Are the questions probing, and do they lead to follow-up questions?
- Are the questions something that can easily be answered by proper research or only answerable by the guest speaker?
- Have you used all of the interrogatives—who, how, why, when, what, and where?

These are always a good base for structuring questions.

A few years ago, a young student had a chronic illness that prevented her from attending classes. She quickly became fatigued and would have to go home. Like most young people, she enjoyed both the social and educational aspects of school. She had a good circle of friends and missed the company, and she was also becoming increasingly bored at home.

The homeroom teacher was concerned about the amount of school she was missing. So he arranged for the family to set up a Skype account, and he set up one in the classroom. Then using the videoconferencing aspect of Skype, the student was able to attend morning classes from the comfort of her home.

Initially, the process was uncomfortable and artificial, but as the student, the teacher, and the class adapted to having her virtual presence in the classroom, she was able to participate more and more in class activities. It was not unusual to see the computer as part of a discussion circle and her voice clearly contributing to group discussions, decisions, and the learning process. The teacher was able to ask her questions and clarify her queries when he was teaching from the front of the room. The process of using Skype in the classroom for this was a success. The student made a satisfactory recovery from her illness and has now returned to school.

Classroom Examples That Cultivate The 21st Century Fluencies

- **Solution Fluency**—Students can use a visual and auditory medium to facilitate discussions related to designing, developing, and refining a solution. *Example:* The Design class uses Skype to talk with an engineer about the design considerations for a bridge-building competition and discuss which design has the highest strength-to-weight ratio.

- **Information Fluency**—Students can conduct primary research and be able to discuss and debate concepts and ideas. *Examples:* The Senior Chemistry class uses Skype to listen to a presentation from an eminent scientist and then have a follow-up question-and-answer session with the presenter.

- **Collaboration Fluency**—Students can collaborate with peers or experts independent of distance and time zones. *Examples:* Foreign Language students use Skype to talk to native language students to practice their pronunciation and conversation skills; students participating in a Flat Classroom project collaborate and report on the effectiveness of current educational practice on the digital generation.

- **Creativity Fluency**—Students can share experiences, ideas, and concepts to gain opinions, critique, and reflection of a creative solution. *Examples:* Design students ask architects to critique their proposals for an assignment related to the design of a new school; as part of their beta testing cycle for refining their solutions, the students interview a land developer.

- **Media Fluency**—Students can consider and discuss various media and approaches to delivering a solution. *Examples:* A teacher who is unable to come to school because of illness within the family, uses Skype to assess and critique a student musical or theatrical performance; students speak with the owner of a design firm to ask questions about design considerations for the school year book.

21st Century Fluency Project

VoIP (Skype) Rubric for Preparation and Planning

This is a rubric for audio and audio/videoconferencing using tools like Skype, Gmail Chat, or Google Wave.

4

User has selected suitable tools and has installed and tested these for use in the conference (blackboards, recorder, and such). Connections are tested prior to the event. A schedule has been communicated and agreed to by all parties. Clear goals for the conference are agreed to by all parties. A plan and key questions are prepared and approved. Suitable resources and links are prepared in advance. Rules and etiquette guidelines are clearly defined.

3

User has selected some suitable tools and installed these for use in the conference (blackboards, recorder, etc.). Connections are tested prior to the event. A schedule has been communicated. Goals for the conference are outlined. A plan and some key questions are prepared. Some resources and links are prepared in advance. Rules and etiquette guidelines are defined.

2

Some connections are tested prior to the event. A schedule has been communicated. Some goals for the conference are outlined. Some key questions are prepared. Rules and etiquette guidelines are outlined.

1

Little preparation is evident. The conference lacks structure. Little consideration for availability, time zones, and such are evident.

21st Century Fluency Project

VoIP (Skype) Rubric for Communication

This is a rubric for audio and audio/videoconferencing using tools like Skype, Gmail Chat, or Google Wave.

4 Rules and etiquette guidelines are clearly defined and adhered to. All communication is clear and articulate (speech, visual, and written) and on task. Users select and use appropriate language that all parties will understand (spoken and written). Speech is clear and appropriately paced and pitched. Suitable standards of etiquette are applied regarding interrupting, turns to speak, use of slang and abbreviation, use of cameras, and prepared materials. Goals and plans of the conference are clearly communicated and adhered to. Suitable notes and/or recording are taken.

3 Rules and etiquette guidelines are stated and mostly adhered to. Most communication is clear and articulate (speech, visual, and written) and mostly on task. The language used is mostly appropriate, and all parties will understand (spoken and written). Speech is mostly clear, and appropriately paced, and appropriately pitched. Rules and etiquette guidelines stated are mostly followed.

2 Rules and etiquette guidelines are stated. Most communication is clear (speech, visual, and written) and mainly on task. The language used is mostly appropriate, and all parties will understand (spoken and written). Slang, regional language, and colloquialisms are used. Speech is mostly clear, but there are issues with pace and pitch. Volume of speech varies. Most rules and etiquette guidelines are followed. There is some interruption and speaking over people. Some notes are taken, but these are of poor quality.

1 Communication is poor, hard to understand, off-task, and inarticulate. Use and selection of language does not aid communication. There is little evidence of rules or etiquette, structure, or planning.

21st Century Fluency Project

VoIP (Skype) Rubric for Reflection

This is a rubric for audio and audio/videoconferencing using tools like Skype, Gmail Chat, or Google Wave.

4
All parties reflect critically on the conference. Reflection is completed without put-downs, sarcasm, or comments of a personal nature. Reflection and review examined appropriately the following: preparation, goals, key questions, process, communications, conversations, and rules and etiquette. Where appropriate, suitable resources, minutes, and notes are developed and distributed. Improvements are identified and actioned.

3
Parties reflect on the conference. Reflection is completed without put-downs, sarcasm, or comments of a personal nature. Reflection and review examined appropriately some of the following: preparation, goals, key questions, process, communications, conversations, and rules and etiquette. Where appropriate, suitable resources, minutes, and notes are distributed. Some areas of improvement are identified and actioned. Some notes and/or recording are taken.

2
There is some limited reflection on the conference. Reflection is general and unstructured. Reflection may be of a personal nature. Minutes and notes are distributed. Some areas of improvement are identified.

1
There is little or no reflection.

21ˢᵗ Century Fluency Project

Question Development Rubric

This is a rubric for developing questions for use in interviews. The emphasis is on questions that are open and probing and are beyond the scope of normal secondary research. These questions will provide the interviewer with insight and clarity. Interviews can be conducted using electronic mediums such as: email; audioconferencing (phone conversations, Skype, and so on); videoconferencing (videoconferencing kits like Lifesize or Polycom, Skype, and so on); online collaboration tools (Elluminate, Adobe Connect, and so on); threaded discussions; face-to-face interviews.

4 The student clearly understands the topic and purpose of the interview. Secondary research is extensive, and the interviewer is well prepared. This is evident in the questions. Questions are open. Questions are focused on the topic or purpose of the interview. Questions are appropriate and suitable for the purpose and interviewee. Questions are structured to flow and have a clear, logical progression. Questions are easily understood and require little or no clarification.

3 The student understands the topic and purpose of the interview. The student has undertaken suitable secondary research, and the interviewer is prepared. Questions are mostly open. Questions are mostly focused on the topic or purpose of the interview. Questions are appropriate and suitable for the purpose and interviewee. Questions have logical flow and progression. Most questions are easily understood, but some questions require clarification.

2 The student has some understanding of the topic and purpose of the interview. The student has undertaken some secondary research but is not fully prepared. Some questions are open, but there are some closed questions. Most questions are focused on the topic or purpose of the interview, but some questions are off-topic or irrelevant. Some questions are inappropriate or unsuitable for the purpose and interviewee. There is some evidence of logical flow and progression, but some lines of questioning have dead ends. Some questions are easily understood, but others require clarification.

1 The student has little understanding of the topic and purpose of the interview. Questions are irrelevant and lack clear focus. The student is not prepared or is poorly prepared and has completed little or no secondary research. Questions are predominantly closed. Few questions are focused on the topic or purpose of the interview. Some questions are distracting. Some questions are inappropriate or unsuitable for the purpose and interviewee. There is little evidence of logical flow and progression, and many lines of questioning have dead ends. Some questions require clarification.

Summary

- Skype is a powerful tool that allows you to enhance your online experience by collaborating and sharing with your friends and peers.

- The Skype software allows you to chat, speak, and have video conversations with one or more people.

- You can connect to other people using Skype or call them directly on their traditional telephone lines.

- Skype also allows you to exchange files and documents using the chat window.

- Essentially, Skype is a powerful tool for keeping in touch.

Questions to Ask

- Why is Skype such an important and economical communication tool for people separated by great distances?

- What is one of the most important aspects of communication that Skype reinforces—one that we don't get in conventional means of communication like phone or email?

- What are some of the more advanced uses of Skype for business or other collaborative settings?

- How is Skype efficient as a classroom tool when you want to have a guest speaker or other special guest?

Resources

Skype Video Tutorial: Skype Community—
  http://forum.skype.com/index.php?showtopic=41492

Skype tutorials—http://skypetutorials.com

EdTechTeacher Skype tutorial—www.edtechteacher.org/skypetutorial.html

How to Get Skype Up and Running—
  http://newley.com/2007/10/08/how-to-use-skype-a-tutorial

Short Takes tutorial: Skype Basics—
  www.scribd.com/doc/5397421/Short-Takes-Tutorial-Skype-Basics

Downloadable PDF Skype tutorial—
  www.educationworld.com/a_tech/techtorial/techtorial107.pdf

Chapter 6
Twitter

> There's a bigger trend I'm seeing; People who used to enjoy blogging their lives are now moving to Twitter.
>
> **Robert Scoble**

Expectations: What Will You Learn?

In this chapter, you will learn about one of the new trends sweeping the Web—Twitter. Twitter is a microblogging tool. You will experiment with Twitter, find friends, and organize feeds that will keep you up-to-date with the latest news, what's happening with your friends, and even gossip.

You will see how Twitter can be a lifeline when you need help and a voice in the dark when things go wrong.

Microblogging Terminology

Blog is a contraction of *web log* and is an online journal that people can subscribe to. A blog can have an audience of one or thousands.

Feed aggregator is a utility or tool that allows you to collect your RSS feeds together in one place and view updates, save interesting posts, and subscribe to and manage your news and information sources. These can either be online tools, such as bloglines (www.bloglines.com) or Google reader (www.google.com/reader), or software installed on your computer such as Feedreader or Flock.

Feeds are online resources such as blogs, web pages, Twitter, and so on that a user can subscribe to in a feed aggregator.

Followers are people who are subscribing to your Twitter posts.

Microblogging is a Web 2.0 tool that allows the user to post short (up to 140 characters long) updates and messages to either a public or private audience.

Protected is where only followers you have approved and accepted can see your posts or Tweets.

Public timeline is publicly viewable messages that are not protected.

RSS is an abbreviation for Really Simple Syndication. RSS is a tool that allows you to subscribe to various online feeds and receive notification when they are updated.

Tweet is a popular name for a user's post or message on the microblogging tool Twitter.

Twitter is a microblogging tool that allows you to aggregate other Twitter feeds and manage your feeds and posts.

URL stands for Universal Resource Locater. A URL is the web address of a page or online resource—www.twitter.com is the URL of Twitter.

Why Do You Tweet?

In an unusual turn of events, Allanah's ever-reliable MacBook© died during an upgrade to the newest version of the operating system. Allanah was well prepared for such an event, having purchased and set up Time Capsule© to back up her MacBook. Unfortunately, or perhaps fortunately, her MacBook had been so reliable that she had never had to restore her computer from the backup.

Unsure of where to start, she turned to Twitter. She posted a quick SOS, explaining that she needed help restoring from Time Capsule. Help appeared in the form of short messages and advice from her followers. The process of restoring her beloved MacBook was quickly sorted and Allanah and her now restored MacBook were reunited.

This vignette is an almost daily occurrence as Twitter users use this short messaging service to quickly draw upon the collective wisdom and knowledge of friends, colleagues, and followers. For many, Twitter forms the hub of their personal learning network (PLN). Twitter is also a social tool that allows you to post brief updates on your activities, share experiences, and exchange web addresses (URLs) or links.

In the silence that followed the devastating earthquake in Sichuan Province in China in May 2008 and in the darkest hours of the 2009 Iranian elections, Twitter was one of the few means of contact with the outside world. In those times of crisis, Twitter provided a lifeline reaching beyond the devastation and the walls of silence to bring us news and calls for help. These were perhaps some of Twitter's finest hours.

What Is Twitter?

Twitter is a microblogging tool. It allows the person sending the Twitter message, to post a short message of up to 140 characters in length to a general audience, addressed to one or more recipients in public view or in a private direct message.

Twitter allows you to subscribe to other people's posts and follow their updates. There are a number of other features of Twitter, including adding tags to posts so they can be searched for. An example of this was the tag added to posts referring to the Iranian elections.

Posts were marked or tagged with #iranelection. Entering this tag in the search field brings up the most recent messages with this tag.

In July 2009, Twitter had 380 million daily hits and 58 million daily visitors.

Why Did We Select Twitter?

Twitter has seen a surge in growth and popularity as more and more people have caught on to the microblogging wave. While on the surface it appears to be shallow and limited, practice has shown a different aspect.

There are also other tools that fill a similar niche, such as Pownce (www.pownce.com) and Jaiku (www.jaiku.com).

How Do You Use Twitter Personally?

To use Twitter, you have to register first. This is a very easy process. First, go to the Twitter site (www.twitter.com). Click on the Get Started—Join link and start the registration process (see Figure 6-1).

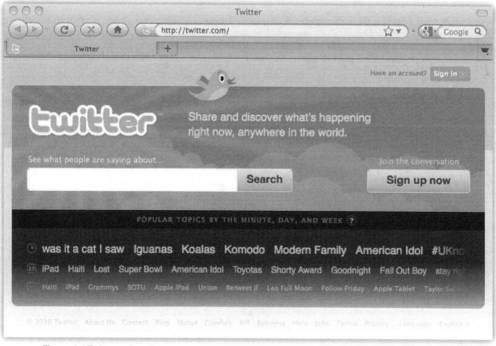

Figure 6-1 *Twitter registration*

The registration requires only a limited amount of your personal information (see Figure 6-2), which includes:

- your name

- the username you would like to use in Twitter

- a password—as with all passwords, it is always recommended that it includes numbers and letters and be at least six characters long

- your email address

Figure 6-2 Account registration

Once you have entered this information, click on the Create my account link, and you are ready to start.

Finding Friends

We have created an account, but who can you talk to? The second step in the Twitter process is to look at your online email accounts and see if any of your contacts are Twitter users. As seen in Figure 6-3, Twitter has access to my gmail account and from there it can locate the members of my contacts list who have Twitter accounts. It will also suggest some high-profile Twitter users to follow as well.

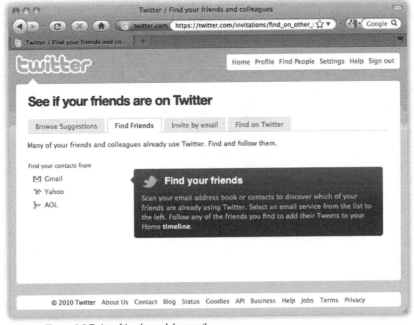

Figure 6-3 Twitter friend search by email

Final Check—A Look at Settings

Under the Settings tab we can add a picture and adjust the various settings for our Twitter account (see Figure 6-4).

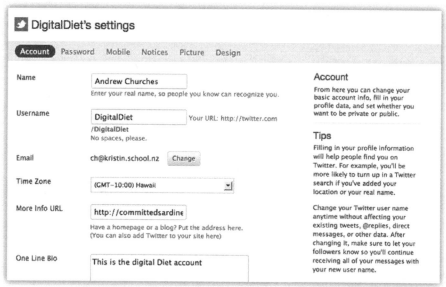

Figure 6-4 *Twitter settings for "Digital Diet"*

Some of the key settings are

- *Time zone*—This lets your followers know what time it is where you are.
- *Location*—Where in the world are you?
- *More info URL*—This is a link to your web site.
- *One-line bio*—This is a brief description of yourself (under 160 characters).

One of the cool options available with Twitter is the ability to update from your cell phone. This can be a useful way of updating your friends on your latest activity (see Figure 6-5).

Figure 6-5 *Twitter message "from the slopes"*

Start Twittering

Now it's time to start Twittering. You just got back from your trip to the mountains. The powder was deep, the runs groomed, and your board tuned, waxed, and the edges sharp. You have posted your photos on Flickr (see Chapter 10) and made a great post on your blog (see Chapter 7). How do you let your friends know you have posted these updates? Simple—*Talk to everyone!* This is a general announcement (see Figure 6-6) where you type your message in the box and send it. It goes to everyone who is subscribed to your updates. If you have not protected your updates, then this message will also appear on the public timeline.

Figure 6-6 *Twitter general announcement*

Next, *shout out to someone*, but everyone can hear (see Figure 6-7). This is where in your message you include the Twitter name of somebody with the @ symbol before it. The message is a specific to @somebody, but it's not a direct message so everyone can see it.

Figure 6-7 *Message to @achurches*

You can also *send a private message*. This uses the direct message feature. Click on the Direct messages link on the navigation bar and you will be able to send a message to just the people you select. Select your recipients from the people you are following. You can also direct message anyone you are not following. Direct messages have an inbox and a box for sent items (see Figure 6-8).

Figure 6-8 *Direct messages*

Replying to a message is easy too. When you get a message you want to reply to, click on the message and select the reply arrow. This will add the sender's name to the message box and you can reply to them (see Figure 6-9).

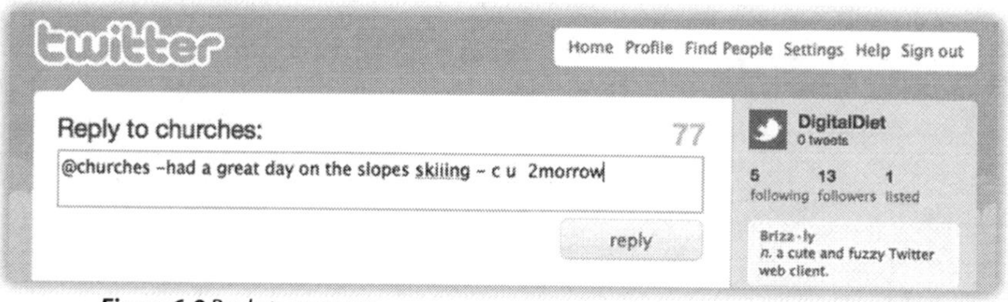

Figure 6-9 *Reply to message*

How do I know if someone has sent me a message? Any messages that contain your user name will be listed and available for you to read when you click on the @username link in the navigation bar (see Figure 6-10).

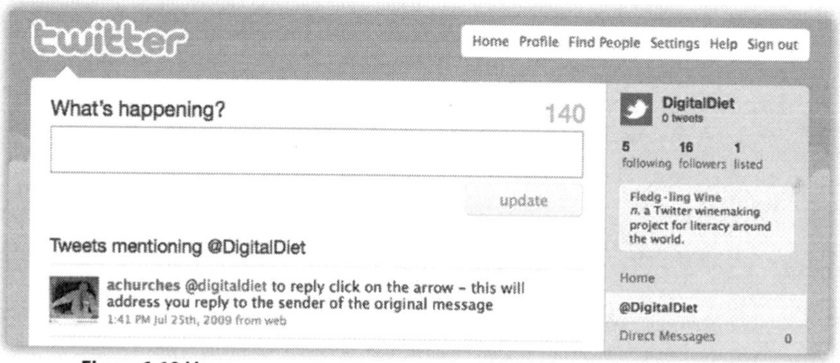

Figure 6-10 *Messages*

Can I save messages? Yes! Click on the message you want to save and then click on the star icon. This will add your message to your favorites. Clicking on the Favorites link will allow you to access these saved messages (see Figure 6-11).

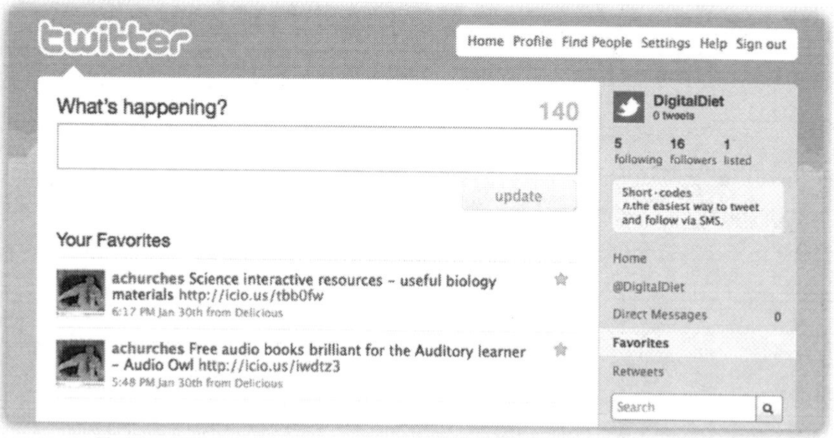

Figure 6-11 *Favorites*

Advanced Uses

- **Twitter from your cell phone.** Twitter, like many social tools, is also available from your cell phone. The process is straightforward and is supported by many telecommunication companies around the world. It is worth checking out. *(http://twitter.com/TwitterMobile)*

- Install a desktop Twitter aggregator. There are a number of these available for both Windows and Mac platforms. They can provide a huge level of functionality at little or no cost and are worth considering. Some of the applications are:

  - *TweetDeck—www.tweetdeck.com*

  - *Twhirl—www.twhirl.org*

  - *Digsby: This application aggregates all of your social networking feeds into one desktop program and is an excellent way to manage your tools— www.digsby.com*

- Send pictures from Twitter. This uses twitpic (twitpic.com) to send a link from your picture to your Twitter feed.

- Tell others about your blog updates using Twitter. Many blogging tools will allow you to update your Twitter feed about recent blog posts. Try Twitterfeed—twitterfeed.com

- Use the hash tag (#) to group and collate tweets. This is a powerful way of structuring your tweets and the responses of your followers. As a teacher using Twitter in the classroom, the hash tags will allow you to organize and coordinate the students' contributions to specific questions, discussions, or topics. For example, students may be revising Romeo and Juliet, so using the hash tag #romeo makes it easy for the students to find all tweets on this topic.

How Do I Use It in a Classroom?

Probably the best example of Twitter in the classroom comes from a brilliant video clip on YouTube by Dr. Monica Rankin. She used it to facilitate the discussion in her classes at the School of Arts and Humanities at UT Dallas. (Watch the video at www.youtube.com/watch?v=6WPVWDkF7U8.)

Dr. Rankin is using Twitter to engage her students. She teaches in a traditional university setting and getting her students to engage and participate in class discussions is hard, with few students being able to contribute. The shy or quiet students did not often participate. Their voices went unheard and their contributions were missed.

By using Twitter, the students had the opportunity to make their comments and opinions heard by the whole audience. Dr. Rankin was able to facilitate the discussion by challenging Twitter posts and answering and posing questions. Distance became less of a problem as she could monitor and respond to tweets from anywhere with an Internet connection.

This model of use is easy to replicate. Using tools like Twitter is fun, engaging, and motivating. In short, it won't even feel like work and the responses from the students will amaze you. Following is a possible process:

- *Class discussion about purpose and ground rules.* Teachers explain the purpose of using Twitter in the classroom and beyond. They develop a set of ground rules with the students by asking them to propose their standards of behavior and use. The teachers help scaffold the discussion by talking about the ground rules for the classroom and classroom discussions. Have the students sign up to their ground rules for behavior—no signature = no membership.

- *Set up those accounts.* In many ways, it is probably easier to have the students set up fresh accounts that are only used for education. This keeps separate their personal and educational use of the tool, protecting privacy and helping to keep the focus on learning. Making the accounts private means only class members—and they have to be invited—can see the updates.

- *Set a schedule and post it.* The teacher must schedule when he or she is going post questions or facilitate discussions. To get engagement, we know that feedback (in this case, comments from the teacher and peers) needs to be timely and appropriate. If you have to wait a day for a comment, you have missed the point of using this tool. Schedule when you are available and then monitor other activity. Act quickly when the ground rules are not followed.

- *Engage the students in process and evaluation.* Student ownership of their learning is one of the most powerful learning processes. Allow them to pose questions and suggest answers and to support their peers and use them as a learning resource. Get the students to tell you how the process and use of Twitter can be improved.

Classroom Examples That Cultivate The 21st Century Fluencies

- **Solution Fluency**—Students can consult their personal learning network for solutions or assistance with the development of a solution. *Examples:* Ask Twitter followers for technical information, such as how to animate a presentation; other followers provide support, encouragement, and suggestions to the learner.

- **Information Fluency**—Students can access a wide range of peers or experts to locate and validate information sources. *Examples:* Students post web site links, online resources, and other materials that they have found useful and view other students posts as they publish them; students using social bookmarking tools to publish their bookmarks also post to Twitter.

- **Collaboration Fluency**—Students can tap into the wisdom of their networks by quickly sharing ideas and concepts with a targeted or broader group of people and obtain their perspectives and suggestions. Example: While writing a story, students use Twitter to collaborate on key points of the plot; use Twitter to brainstorm possible solutions to a problem.

- **Creativity Fluency**—Students can obtain suggestions, recommendations, critiques, and feedback from a diverse base. *Examples:* Draw upon a wide range of perspectives while proposing a solution to a design problem by soliciting learning networks for materials, web sites, and suggestions; use the 140 characters of Twitter to summarize a classical novel, an historical event, or a political figure.

- **Media Fluency**—Students can evaluate the limitations and strengths of short messaging service. *Example:* Use Twitter to compare the advantages of informal short messaging services with the more formal use of email.

Summary

- So that's Twitter. For some people, Twitter is a key component in what they call their personal learning network. For others, it's a way to stay in touch and up-to-date with friends and colleagues and even receive updates from celebrities. For others, it's a voice in the dark when everything else is silent.

- Twitter allows you to send and receive short messages in a private or public forum. To save these, tag them with keywords and search.

- It allows you to follow politicians, celebrities, and even your neighbors as they tweet their way through each day.

Questions to Ask

- Who should be seeing my updates? Should I protect them?

- Do I know the people I am following and who are following me?

- When should I Twitter? Is twittering at work appropriate?

- Ask yourself questions before you post such as, *"What should I say?"*, or *"Is this too much information?"*

Resources

The Commoncraft show is a great source of resources. Have a look at these two brilliant Twitter videos—Twitter in Plain English (www.commoncraft.com/twitter) and Twitter Search in Plain English (www.commoncraft.com/twitter-search)

Twitter's Help page is a very useful resource that answers many of the questions you will have and includes a useful video too—http://help.twitter.com/portal

For a starter sheet on how to use this tool try— http://edorigami.wikispaces.com/Starter+Sheets

Twitter tutorial on Slideshare—www.slideshare.net/Griner/the-twitter-tutorial

WebDesignerDepot's Ultimate Guide to Everything Twitter— www.webdesignerdepot.com/2009/03/the-ultimate-guide-for-everything-twitter/

Chapter 7
Blogging with Blogger

> Getting information off the Internet is like taking a drink from a fire hydrant.
>
> **Mitchell Kapor**

 ## Expectations: What Will You Learn?

This chapter is going to introduce you to blogging. We will talk about what blogging is, where it came from, who blogs, and why.

We will look at Blogger as our tool for blogging but also look at several other tools that allow us to create blogs. Step by step, we will work our way through the process of creating a blog through to our first post. Blogging is exciting, varied, and dynamic. It provides a medium to share your thoughts, state your opinions, and air your ideas. Whether your blog is a personal and private diary just for you or it has a following of multitudes, blogging is for everyone.

Blogging Terminology

Blogger has a twofold meaning. A blogger is a person who writes a blog and is also the name of Google's free blogging tool.

WordPress is a company that hosts blogs and provides brilliant blog hosting software.

Blog is a contraction of the term *web log*. A blog is an online application that allows users to post (or load) text, images, and other materials to their sites. Other readers may also be given permission to leave comments.

Moderate is when comments left by blog readers are checked by the blog owner or moderator before they are made public.

Post is where an entry or update in your blog published.

RSS is an abbreviation for Really Simple Syndication. RSS is a tool that allows you to subscribe to various online feeds and receive notification when these are updated.

RSS aggregator is a tool that allows you to subscribe to the updates from blogs you follow. The aggregator can be an online tool, such as bloglines, or a tool that has been installed on your computer, such as Feedreader.

WYSIWYG is an abbreviation for What You See Is What You Get. This phrase describes tools that let you enter text and format it in the style that it will appear on the screen or when printed out. A word processor such as Microsoft Word or Apple's Pages is described as being a WYSIWYG word processor. With a WYSIWYG editor, you do not need to know any code, like HTML, JavaScript, and such, to produce web pages.

Tags are keywords used to classify your blog posts. Users will often use tags or keywords to sort or search through all of your posts.

Why Did We Select Blogger?

Blogger is another one of the wide selection of tools available from Google. Blogger allows us to use one user ID and password to access several key tools. There are several service providers that offer free basic and advanced blogging services, such as:

- www.blogger.com—This is Google's blogging service.
- http://wordpress.com—This is another free blogging service powered by the widely used WordPress. The basic service is free but premium features will cost you a subscription.
- http://edublogs.org—This is a favorite of the authors and the wider education community. They host Andrew's education blog (http://edorigami.edublogs.org). They use the WordPress server, but are only available for educators. Free for the basic account.
- www.typepad.com—This is a subscription-based service that offers a wide range of features.

There are many other alternatives, and a quick search for comparisons of blogging services will yield some excellent reviews.

What Is It?

A blog such as Google Blog (see Figure 7-1) can be as simple as a diary or as complex as the public face for an organization. A blog allows you to interact with your audience.

Figure 7-1 *Google Blog*

But what is a blog? It is a web page that you can easily create without having to know any complex code or programming. Most blog editors are called WYSIWYG because the product (blog page or post) you produce looks almost exactly like the text and images you entered in the editor.

All blog posts are dated and blog posts are arranged in date order from the most recent to the oldest. Some blogs will allow more than one person to author or write blog posts or entries, which is a common feature when organizations and companies use blogs.

Why Do You Blog?

At 7:15 pm, Andrew touches down in Memphis and catches the transfer bus to his hotel. He logs on to the free wireless in the hotel and blogs about his trip. He uploads some photographs from the plane and hotel. He publishes the post. Andrew's family and friends receive an update in their online RSS aggregator, Bloglines, telling them that Andrew had made a new post. They can all see his latest post and are able to leave comments. As he continues his trip, he creates additional updates (called posts).

Blogs can be personal journals and diaries or they can be the outside face of an organization. Many major corporations such as Google have a blog they use to maintain conversations with their customers.

Some blogs, like Lifehacker, are groups that contribute to a wide variety of topics (see Figure 7-2).

Figure 7-2 *Lifehacker*

How Do You Use It Personally?

You could sign up to one of many blog service providers, but to illustrate this process we will use Blogger, which is the blogging tool provided by Google.

So where do you start? Open up a web browser such as Internet Explorer, Mozilla's Firefox, or Apple's Safari or Opera, and enter this address in the URL search bar: *www.blogger.com/start*. This takes us to the start screen (Figure 7-4 on the next page), where we begin the process of creating our brand new blog. (Once we have created the blog, we would use the "Sign in to Blogger" option, shown in Figure 7-3 at right).

Figure 7-3 *Sign in to Blogger*

Figure 7-4 *Blogger home*

A Consideration

Like many online services, Blogger will give you the option of saving your password using the Remember Me tick box. This is a great time saver but should only be done on machines that are not used by the public—*never* in an Internet cafe!

Once you have clicked on the Create a Blog link, you have started a three-step process. The steps are:

- Create an account—This stage gathers basic information about you and establishes your password and security information.

- Name the blog—This is a key step. The name of the blog can have huge importance if you are going to use the blog commercially.

- Choose a template—This stage allows you to choose and customize a template for the appearance of your blog.

Step 1: Create an Account

This stage sets up your identity and password (see Figure 7-5). You will be asked to:

- enter an existing email address—Ideally, use the gmail one you will set up in the appendix. You will be asked to re-enter this to confirm it is entered correctly.

- enter a password—This is at least three characters long, but that would be a very weak password. We would recommend that a password contain eight characters with a combination of numbers and letters. You can measure the strength of your password (see Figure 7-5).

- Display name—This is the name you will use to sign your posts. This could be your actual name or a pseudonym you choose. It is important to consider the meaning the name may have and the implications of this.

- Word verification—This is a security process that helps to prevent computer programs called "bots" from creating blogs.

- Don't forget the terms and conditions. Then click Continue to proceed to the second stage.

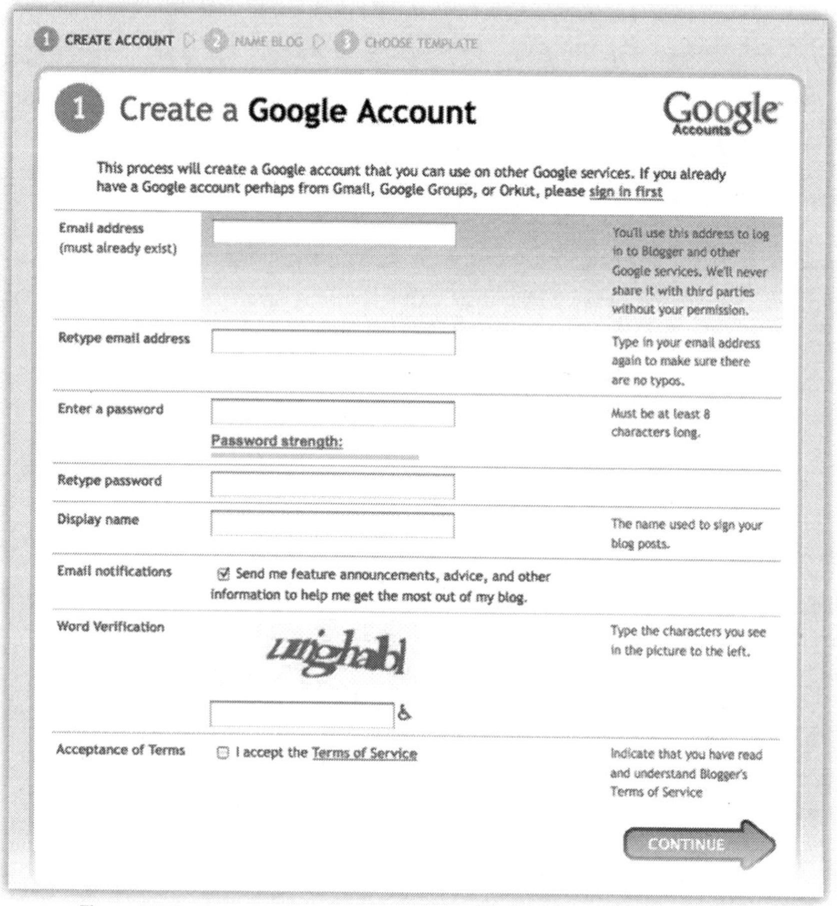

Figure 7-5 Create account

Step 2: Name the Blog

Names are important, especially if the audience for your blog is a large one. You need a title for your blog and this should be similar to your web address. The name you choose will be part of the web address or URL that people access the blog from.

For example, if you call your blog The Digital Diet, the URL will be http://thedigitaldiet.blogger.com (see Figure 7-6).

Figure 7-6 Name your blog

Important

You need to check the availability of your name. Sometimes other people have already claimed the name you want. Blogger will suggest alternatives based on the title of your blog. Again there is a security question to ensure you are not a computer program.

Step 3: Choose a Template

In this step, you will set the theme of your blog. Is it bright and bubbly or gothic and dark, playful and fun or serious and professional? Blogger (and almost all other blogging services) provides you with a selection of prepared templates you can use and customize.

Browse through the selections and pick one that suits you, your blog, and your message or theme. Click the Continue button and you have created your blog (see Figure 7-7). It's as simple as that!

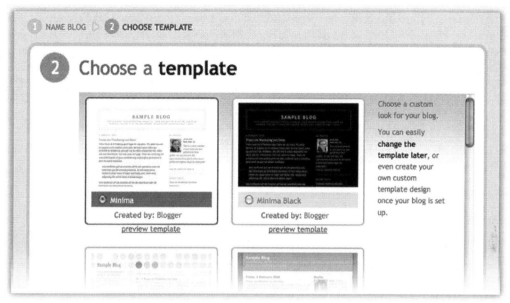

Figure 7-7 *Pick and save template*

Let's Start Blogging

So, how do you do it? The answer is pretty straightforward. You type in the text you want and add in the formatting and layout (see Figure 7-8).

Figure 7-8 *Blogging window*

The formatting tools that you'll find on the toolbar at the top of your blog screen are simple and easy to use. With these tools, you can:

- select your font and font size
- use simple text decorations like bold and italic
- choose font color
- insert a link to another web page
- align your text to left, center, right, or justify (where the text is evenly aligned across the space)
- use bullet points
- insert images and other media
- use the spell checker and eraser found on the toolbar.

It is always a good idea to have an outline and plan of what you want to say. Again, I like the 5P rule of planning:

The 5P Rule

Proper **P**lanning **P**revents **P**oor **P**erformance

Let's Add Some Pictures

You can upload a picture from your computer by clicking on the Choose button and then finding the image on your computer or from a suitable site on the Web (see Figure 7-9). Then select your alignment and image size, and click Upload image.

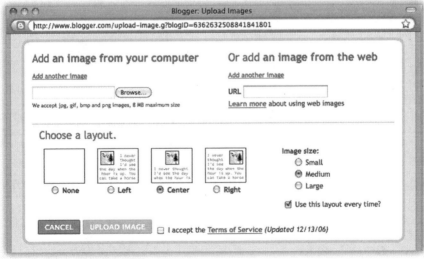

Figure 7-9 *Choose image*

Often you will want to make links to other web pages or web sites. This process is straightforward. Select the text (or image) that you want to be your link and then click on the Link button on the toolbar.

Figure 7-10 shows the finished product. The background is the theme I selected when I set up. As you can see, the post is dated and is displayed in date order of most recent posts first. You can change the theme and other settings for your posts, including privacy, from the Settings tab in your Blogger workspace.

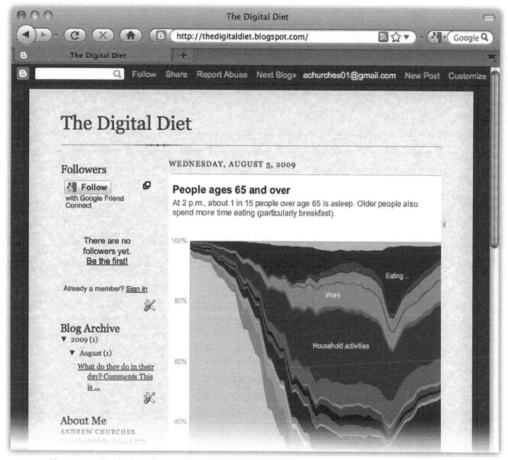

Figure 7-10 *Finished product*

How Do I Share My Blog?

The easiest way is to email your friends and colleagues with the blog's address. When they visit your site, they will have the option of subscribing to your blog feed using RSS. Blogger uses Atom to subscribe people to blogs. You may need to set up a blog aggregator to collect all your blog feeds.

Figure 7-11 *Advanced options*

Advanced Uses

At this point, there are some advanced options that experienced users can set up (see Figure 7-11). These include setting up a specific domain name. For example, you may have purchased a domain name like www.Groundflight.com. In the advanced options, you can use this domain name as the address for your blog.

If you have an existing Blogger blog, you can import your posts and materials into the one you have just created.

How Do I Use It in a Classroom?

Ian is an information technology and computer studies teacher. One aspect of the course he teaches is current issues in information technology. In the final examination, his students will be presented with a previously unseen news article and asked to:

- identify the issue
- present information on the IT background to it
- analyze and evaluate the impact of the issue on society
- propose a solution to the issue and evaluate it.

These are obviously skills and processes that require practice and feedback to develop. The students' learning will be enhanced if they can see other responses and approaches to the news article and be provided with feedback from a variety of sources and perspectives, not just their teacher.

Ian decides to use a blog as a solution to this. He creates a Blogger blog and gives his blog a suitable name. He then distributes the URL to his students and the head of his department. The blog permissions are set so it requires comments to be moderated.

Ian then locates suitable articles and includes extracts of these in his blog posts. He clearly defines the aspect he is examining in each post. He asks the students to read and identify the issue and its underlying IT system or to provide a brief background of the IT system in the article, and to analyze and evaluate the impact of the issue on society or propose a solution.

The students are required to address the task proposed and use the comment feature of the blog to present their answer for homework. Ian collects all the answers and moderates these at one time. These students are then required to comment constructively on their peers' work. This develops a threaded discussion that Ian and the students benefit from.

Ian has established a clear set of rules for appropriate and acceptable use. These students are aware that inappropriate comments and posts will carry severe consequences. Because all comments are moderated and invisible until approved, Ian can ensure the safety of his students by checking each and every comment posted.

Classroom Examples That Cultivate The 21st Century Fluencies

- **Solution Fluency**—Students can present and publish in a medium where people can easily comment and critique them. *Examples:* Students use their personal blogs to journal the learning process; post reflective journals on a blog and share these reflections with a teacher who uses the comments to provide feedback and suggestions as well as to modify teaching and learning strategies.

- **Information Fluency**—Students can post findings and sources through a medium where others can validate them and offer alternative perspectives through comments. *Examples:* Use blogging to reflect on a learning experience; use blogging to publish information and research as it relates to a research paper or class presentation.

- **Collaboration Fluency**—Students can invite others to share ideas, processes, suggestions, comments, and feedback. *Examples:* Use a collaborative blog that allows each student to post entries to brainstorm, collaborate, and reflect on a group project; offer peers feedback, critique, and comment.

- **Creativity Fluency**—Students can use a blog as a way to publish products, solutions, or media. *Example:* Students post a storyboard and script for a short film, then invite peers and teachers to offer comment and suggestions about the development process.

- **Media Fluency**—Students will compare the limitations and strengths of blogging as a media delivery solution. *Example:* Create a blog comment to answer challenging questions about the genre, plots, and characters of television episodes from online media sharing sites.

21st Century Fluency Project

Blog Commenting Rubric for Construction

This is a rubric for blog commenting. It examines the process of commenting on blog posts. At the simplest level, the student is showing understanding; at higher levels, the student is evaluating the post and making critical comments and reflections.

4 Spelling and grammatical errors are rare. Comments have structure and flow and are constructed to enhance readability. Comments contain appropriate links, uploaded files, or images. Sources are acknowledged and other posts and comments are linked to.

3 Few spelling and grammatical errors. Comments have structure and the entry flows. The comments contain sentences or paragraphs. The comments contain appropriate links, uploaded files, or images. Comments refer to other posts or comments.

2 Some poor spelling and grammatical errors. Comments have some structure, but the entry does not flow. The comments contain several sentences and may contain a link or image. The construction is mainly formal, containing few abbreviations or text-style language.

1 Poor spelling and grammatical errors. Short one or two sentences. Lacks structure or flow. Written in informal language, abbreviations, or text-style language. Student makes comments that are inappropriate or unacceptable. Comments are not related to the post or are of a personal nature.

21st Century Fluency Project

Blog Commenting Rubric for Understanding/Evaluation

This is a rubric for blog commenting. It examines the process of commenting on blog posts. At the simplest level, the student is showing understanding; at higher levels, the student is evaluating the post and making critical comments and reflections.

4 The comments show insight, depth, and evaluation. They are connected with original posts and subsequent comments. Entries are relevant with links to supporting material. Personal opinion is expressed in an appropriate style and is clearly related to the thread or post. The comments or posts show a level of evaluation and consider in some depth the outcomes, impacts, or effects of the posts or comments.

3 The comments show insight and depth and are connected with posts and/or comments. Entries may contain some irrelevant material. Personal opinion is expressed in an appropriate style. Considers impact or outcome as a result of the post. Shows some evaluation.

2 Simple comments show some insight and depth and are connected with original post or a comment. The comments are short and may contain some irrelevant material. Offers some personal comments or opinions that may not be on task. Shows some understanding.

1 Simple comments lack insight or depth or are superficial. The entry is short and frequently irrelevant to the key question, original post, or concept. Does not express opinion clearly. Student makes comments that are inappropriate or unacceptable. Comments are not related to the post or are of a personal nature.

Summary

- In this chapter we have looked at why you would set up a blog and looked at some blogging hosts that offer free services.

- We have used Blogger, Google's blogging service, to create our blog and worked through the process of setting up and customizing it.

- We have written a post and then viewed the post we have published to the Web.

Questions to Ask

- Who do I want to read my blog, and how will I control access to it?

- What is the purpose of my blog?

- How do I get people to read it?

- How much personal information am I revealing?

- Is it acceptable to name my friends and colleagues?

- Have I asked permission or acknowledged the source of my images?

Resources

The Commoncraft show is a great source of information in a simple and straightforward format. Here are two brilliant shorts videos that will explain RSS and blogging—www.commoncraft.com/rss_plain_english and www.commoncraft.com/blogs

This is a blog about setting up a blog. It's a great resource put together by Richard Byrne—www.freetech4teachers.com/2009/08/how-to-week-day-2-setting-up-blog.html

Blog Basics List of Tutorials for Blogging—www.blogbasics.com/blog-tutorial-1-1.php

An extensive list of information on blogging—www.blog-tutorials.com

How to Create a Blog Site—www.siteground.com/tutorials/blog

Problogger Tutorial Listing—www.problogger.net/archives/2004/11/19/free-blog-tutorials

Chapter 8
Social Networking

> One loyal friend is worth ten thousand relatives.
>
> **Euripides**

 Expectations: What Will You Learn?

We're going on a social networking adventure. You will create your own Facebook account, find and connect with some of your friends who also have accounts, create an event, and identify your friends in photos you upload.

Social Networking Terminology

Tag in Facebook is how you identify someone in a photo.

Status update is a posting of any combination of text, pictures, videos, links, and event invitations.

Wall is a page on Facebook that contains all your personal status updates as well as comments by your friends.

Friend is someone with whom you are connected by mutual consent.

Friend request is a message from a prospective friend asking for a mutual connection.

News feed is the home page of your Facebook account, listing your posts and the posts of your friends.

Notifications are updates sent to you by Facebook, such as the status of a friend request or a direct message from a friend or group you belong to.

What Is Facebook?

Facebook is a free social networking web site. Users join networks that are organized by various categories, such as by city, social group, or region. Users share their thoughts, photos, links, and more, writing on their wall or their friend's wall. It is a way to keep in touch with people and make new friends, as well as discover what is going on in your community or any area of personal interest. In 2009, compete.com ranked Facebook as the most used social network worldwide. There are more than 250 million active users.

Why Did We Select Facebook?

Facebook is by far the fastest growing social networking tool, and it has been broadly adopted by students, making it the most appropriate tool to demonstrate in this book.

Why Do You Use Facebook?

Joe just graduated and moved to a new community. He wants to keep in contact with his friends and family, who are now spread across the country. At the same time, he wants to get comfortable with his new home.

Through Facebook, he is able to share videos and photos with his friends and family, see what's on their minds with status updates, and share his own thoughts. He joins the local network and finds an arts group that posts what's happening in the local music scene.

Through these posts he finds out about an open mic night at a local coffee house and decides to attend. There he meets Jamie, a fellow dog lover who also recently moved to town, and they start dating. Through Facebook, he shares the news of his new relationship and his life adventures with friends and family. Joe and Jamie join a local dog lover's Facebook group and find out about the dog-friendly picnics at a local park on Sunday afternoons. They attend one and make new friends. Joe and Jamie get married, their dog has puppies, and they live happily ever after.

How Do You Use Facebook Personally?

First, you must set up an account. It's free and requires very little information. The home page is at www.facebook.com. On the home page is the sign-up form where you enter your name, email, a password, your gender, and your birthday (see Figure 8-1). Your gender and birthday are required to ensure age-appropriate access to content. You can hide this information in your personal settings if you wish.

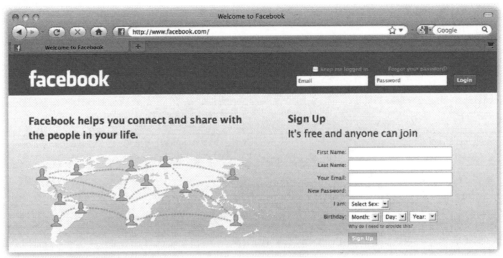

Figure 8-1 *Facebook sign-up page*

Once you register, you will receive an email confirmation request to ensure the authenticity of your account. Clicking the link in the email will confirm your account. You can then sign in and start updating your information and looking for friends.

The simple step of entering your email address may find friends that have already requested a link to you (see Figure 8-2).

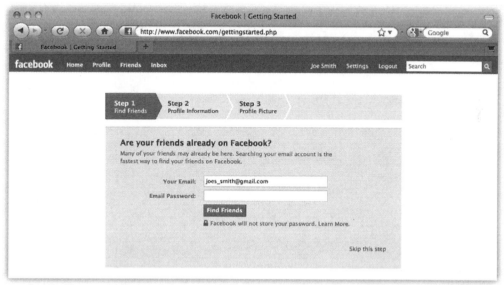

Figure 8-2 Finding friends

The next step of entering your high school, post-secondary, and company information may also instantly find people you are familiar with (see Figure 8-3).

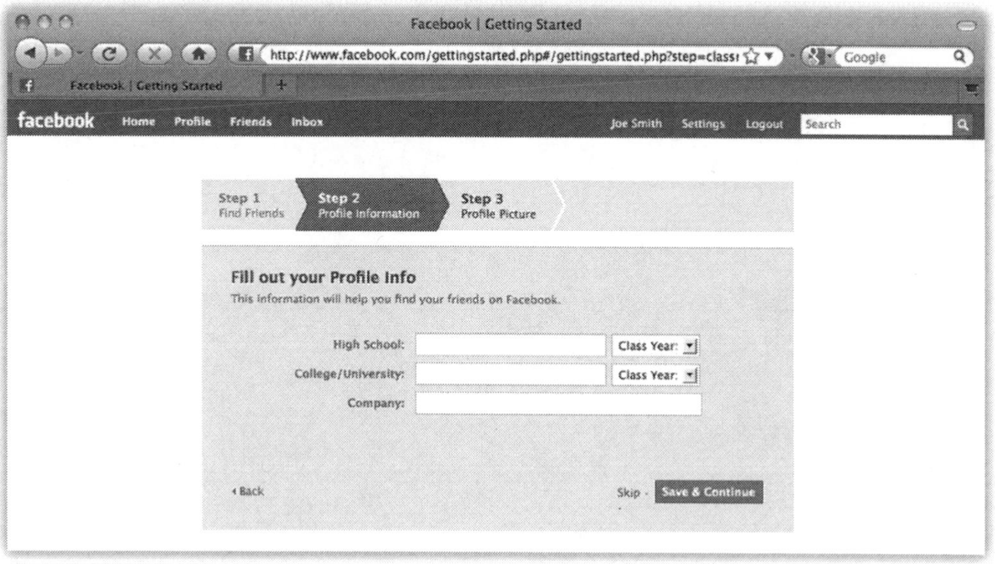

Figure 8-3 School/company information

You can now upload a photo of yourself or take one with your webcam (see Figure 8-4). A picture is really helpful. Often when you search for a friend, you'll find dozens of people with the same name. Having a photo attached makes it a lot easier to find others and for them to find you. Just for fun, after you upload your photo, type your name into the search field on the top right of the page. You'll be surprised how many of you there are!

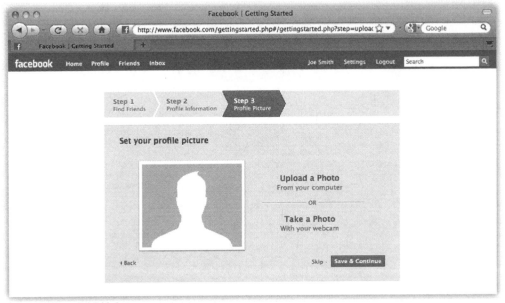

Figure 8-4 *Add photo*

Next, click on your Profile button in the navigation bar, next to your Home button (see Figure 8-5). Here you can fill in a lot of information, but all of this is optional. Only fill in as much as you are comfortable having other people know about you.

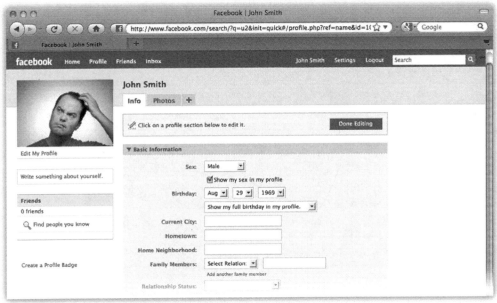

Figure 8-5 *Profile information*

Let's find some friends! Use the search bar on the top right and type in the name of the person you are looking for. As previously mentioned, you'll be surprised how many people share the same name, and the photos come in handy. In Figure 8-6, I find the Lee Crockett I'm looking for and click the Add as Friend button to request the mutual link.

Figure 8-6 *Find friends*

Your prospective friend will receive a friend request, and so will you when someone else requests you as a friend. You can either Confirm or Ignore the request. Once confirmed, your new friend's activities will appear on your wall. You'll see their status updates, what other people write on their wall, photos that they upload or are tagged in, and more.

After someone confirms a friend request, a list of suggestions for possible friends also appears on the right side of your home page. Facebook is finding friends of friends that you may have something in common with.

You will receive notifications by email (check your settings) and also at the bottom of your home page (for example, when your new friends confirm).

You can keep searching and adding friends or areas of special interest. Maybe you're a fan of U2. If so, search for them and join their page (see Figure 8-7). There are thousands of pages for groups and activities on a local, national, and international level. This is what social networking is all about—connecting with friends and making new ones.

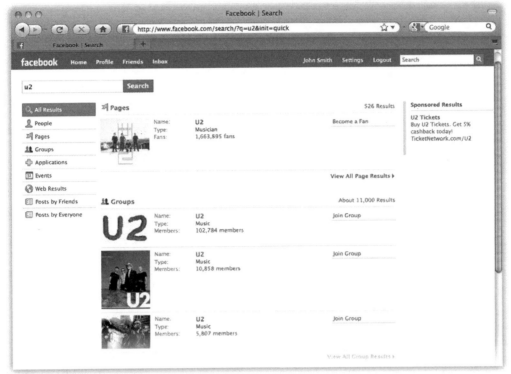

Figure 8-7 *U2 home page*

Now that you are connected to all your friends, it's time to start interacting and letting them know what you're up to. This is what the status update is for. There are no rules—you can type whatever is on your mind. It might be something as simple as, "Mmm . . . coffee" or as profound as, "Today I realized that a friend is someone who knows the song in your heart and can sing it to you when you've forgotten the words."

Once you've been on Facebook for a while you'll see what we mean by "no rules." Some of the best chatter is in the form of comments on your status update. Status updates can be just text or you can add a photo, a video, or a link (see Figure 8-8).

Figure 8-8 *Status update*

In Figure 8-8, Joe is talking about a great web site he's discovered in his status. First he enters the text about the site. Next, he clicks on the link icon and enters the web site address as www.committedsardine.com (see Figure 8-9).

Figure 8-9 *Link to committedsardine.com*

When he clicks the Attach button, Facebook visits the site and scans if for images and text, and automatically creates a preview (see Figure 8-10).

Figure 8-10 *Web site preview*

Clicking the Share button posts these links to your wall, and all your friends will be able to see them on their news feed. Let's look at how to create an event. It could be something formal like a concert or something as informal as a BBQ. First enter the text like before (see Figure 8-11).

Figure 8-11 *Enter text for event*

Then click the event button (the little calendar icon). After entering the date and other information, the event is posted to your wall and everyone is automatically invited (see Figure 8-12).

Figure 8-12 *Invitation to event*

Clicking on the title The Awesome Summer BBQ will take you to a special page for the event, which was automatically created when you created the event (see Figure 8-13).

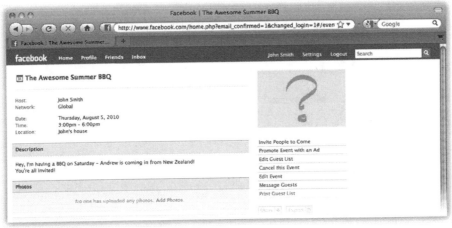

Figure 8-13 *Event page*

Your friends can RSVP so you'll know how many burgers to buy, and after the event everyone can post their photos and videos or make comments so you'll remember the good times.

Posting photos is something that you'll do often with Facebook—either in events such as the one described previously or through your status updates. The photo will appear on your wall as in Figure 8-14.

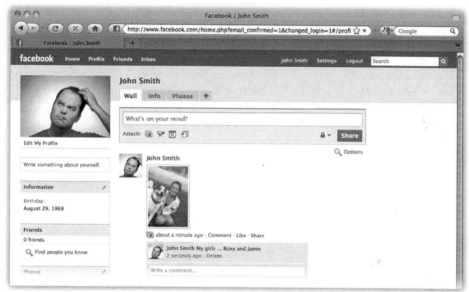

Figure 8-14 *Photo on wall*

A great feature of Facebook photos is the ability to tag or identify people in the photos. Once you upload a photo, clicking on it will allow you to edit the tags (see Figure 8-16). When you do, the photo is now connected to your friend and his or her friends will be able to see your picture as well.

Figure 8-16 *Tagging photos*

Advanced Uses

One of the features of Facebook that has created its mass appeal is applications. These add-ons extend Facebook's functionality immeasurably. There are many applications and advanced uses, and the list keeps growing every day. The following are a just few:

- Download a whole photo album using this Firefox add-on—http://addons.mozilla.org/en-US/firefox/addon/8442
- Share your Flickr photos on Facebook with this URL—www.keebler.net/flickr2facebook
- Update your Facebook status, as well as that of your other social networking sites, all at the same time—http://ping.fm
- Schedule messages to go out in the future—http://sendible.com
- Hide Facebook ads using Facebook Cleaner—http://userscripts.org/scripts/show/27121
- Automatically post your WordPress blog posts to Facebook—http://wordpress.org/extend/plugins/wordbook

How Do I Use It in a Classroom?

Since Facebook is primarily geared toward social interaction, it's a good tool to use for building the working relationships between both students and teachers and can be a great resource in making learning enjoyable and productive.

For example, Facebook's unique sharing interface can enable students to share information and discoveries while engaged in collaborative ventures. It can also be used to post a record of progress that can be viewed by instructors as the students engage in various solo or group projects. They can create limited user profiles with controlled settings for viewing only by selected friends, as well as profiles for the groups they are working in.

For teachers, it can be a great organizational tool. Facebook profiles allow them to oversee course rosters and classes by creating Facebook groups, make more specific lists for course management, host group discussions, and post news and make announcements—all relevant to their specific curriculum content. They can also profile themselves and the courses they teach for viewing by the student body. In a broader sense, Facebook is wonderful for students and teachers to connect with one another by sharing thoughts and opinions, posting photos and video, publishing notes (similar to blogging), and creating a true sense of a "classroom community" in their school.

Imagination is your only limitation for using many of these tools. Facebook has so many possibilities and we'll outline a few for you. However, there are two things that we want to mention. First, and this applies to all the tools we've discussed, don't think you need to know everything. Your best resource is your students. Ask them how you can use these tools in the classroom. They will have a bunch of excellent suggestions— listen to them. They are the experts with this stuff!

Second, and most important, create a separate user account for you as a teacher. Don't use your personal login with your students. You don't want them knowing your friends or following your updates. We have corporate and personal accounts for all these tools, and so should you if you intend to network with your students.

The following are some possible uses for Facebook in the classroom:

- Make friends lists of students by class or project. Then you can message everyone involved at the same time.

- Create groups and have each class or project join that group. This is a mini-community with a specific focus.

- Share photos—students can upload class photos to the group. This really creates a sense of community and belonging.

- Publish notes within your groups and tag students. You can include notes from the class, your thoughts, or a review of what happened that day.

- Use status updates often. Let them know what you're doing or thinking.

- Share videos. If your class is creating videos as part of a class project, upload and share them with the group. This also becomes an idea resource for next year's students.

- Show examples. Through photos or posts you can share resources or publish examples of great work. Give your students something to aim at and exceed.

- Use Courses (http://apps.facebook.com/courses). Here you can actually create courses within Facebook! Create assignments, make announcements, post files, and facilitate discussions.

- Research apps like DoResearch4me for easy information searches—http://apps.facebook.com/doresearchforme

- Get Homework Help for assistance from other students or teachers—www.facebook.com/apps/application.php?id=10425910091

- Create flashcards—http://apps.facebook.com/flashcard

Classroom Examples That Cultivate The 21st Century Fluencies

- **Solution Fluency**—Students can collaborate in the design and development of a solution with with peers in several time zones to compose to compose a global project. *Example:* Students can collaborate asynchronously on the composition of a short video clip that summarizes their aspect of a group project; share documents, storyboards, resources, and materials to a central location provided by a social networking tool.

- **Information Fluency**—Students can actively participate and use a medium to collaborate and validate ideas and concepts. Facilitates the exchange and online storage of ideas, resources, and materials. *Example:* Students can present arguments that validate or invalidate materials presented on a social networking site, providing information sources to support their conclusions.

- **Collaboration Fluency**—Students can actively participate in both synchronous and asynchronous collaboration spaces, including instant messaging or chat, wall posts, calendars, and blog entries. *Examples:* Develop a schedule for completing a community service project using an online calendar; collaborate on aspects of the service project with peers via instant messaging, chat, or wall posts; create blog entries to reflect on the service project throughout the semester.

- **Creativity Fluency**—Students can exchange concepts and ideas in a medium that allows the invited parties to comment and critique. *Examples:* The teacher sets up groups of specific students and asks them to use these spaces to share concepts and designs. The groups limit access to the spaces to members only, allowing the students to develop solutions and materials in private and controlled spaces.

- **Media Fluency**—Students can address the same topic in a single space by embedding a variety of media ranging from video to music, blogs to SMS style comments, and images to posts in a single platform. They can compare and contrast the materials posted. *Examples:* Create a multimedia presentation about an environmental issue in a social networking space using videos, images, blogs, or wall posts to present ideas and solutions; use comments to compare and critique the materials presented by peers.

Summary

- The main concept behind social networking is connectivity. The more you tag people, make entries, and join groups, the more people you'll be connected to.

- It is an excellent way to stay in touch with friends and make new ones. Many people only use Facebook as viewers, but it is not just for consumption—it is a social network.

- You will get far more out of the experience if you post updates, comments, and photos—don't be shy!

Questions to Ask

- Do I want my page to be visible by anyone or only my friends?

- Do I want to accept friend requests from people I don't know?

- How much information about myself am I comfortable sharing with my friends, my family, or new friends?

Resources

Facebook Tutorials—www.allfacebook.com/facebook-tutorials

EHow: How to Use Facebook—www.ehow.com/videos-on_108_use-facebook.html

FacebookAdvice.com—http://facebookadvice.com/tag/facebook-tutorials

Extensive resource for Facebook tutorial—www.mahalo.com/how-to-use-facebook

A list of Facebook applications for students and teachers—
www.collegedegree.com/library/college-life/15-facebook-apps-perfect-for-online-education

32 Ways to Use Facebook in Business—
http://webworkerdaily.com/2009/07/21/32-ways-to-use-facebook-for-business

Downloadable PDF on Facebook classroom uses—
http://org.elon.edu/CATL/conference/documents/FacebookEducation.pdf

This web site has 20 great tips, several of them are things you'll want to do—
www.hongkiat.com/blog/20-facebook-tipstricks-you-might-not-know

10 privacy settings every Facebook user should know—
www.allfacebook.com/2009/02/facebook-privacy

More great tips and tricks—www.switched.com/2008/11/13/facebook-101-25-tips-and-tricks

10 Facebook tips for power users—
www.pcworld.com/article/161688/ten_facebook_tips_for_power_users.html

Chapter 9

VoiceThread

> Good communication is as stimulating as black coffee, and just as hard to sleep after.
>
> **Anne Morrow Lindbergh**

 Expectations: What Will You Learn?

In this chapter, we are going to bring together the power of images and voice, add in text, and create a multimedia presentation using VoiceThread. You will sign up to VoiceThread, set up your profile, upload or link to online images, and add voice commentary and text captions as you construct an exciting and interactive multimedia presentation. VoiceThread is a simple and straightforward approach to producing exciting and dynamic online multimedia presentations.

VoiceThread Terminology

Comments are voice or text comments that you add to your VoiceThread as you are creating it. Other people can add comments using voice, text, or webcam to your threads. These usually have to be moderated.

Doodler is a drawing tool that you can use on your VoiceThreads.

Export means to save your VoiceThread as a file on your computer for playback through your iPod, computer, cell phone, or other digital device.

Moderating is the process of approving the comments that have been left on your VoiceThread by other viewers. Approved comments can be listened to or viewed by all the other visitors to your site.

Server is the central computer or computers that host or store the VoiceThread applications and your uploaded images and files.

Slide show is a progression of images and text used to convey a message.

Upload means to take images or audio files and load them onto the VoiceThread server.

What Is VoiceThread?

VoiceThread is one of a number of tools that allows users to create exciting online slide shows that combine images, video, text, and voice.

Just like most products available on the Web, there are different levels of privacy available to you. You can set your VoiceThread to be public or private as required.

The basic version of VoiceThread we will be using is free, but even the instructional version, which includes up to 100 accounts, online publishing work, and great student management software, costs USD $60 per year.

Why Did We Select VoiceThread?

VoiceThread is a powerful tool that offers a wide range of feature that you can use in the classroom or personally. The ability to add a spoken narration and to leave voice comments while still having the functionality of a slide show tool adds another dimension to learning. A basic VoiceThread account is free, and the educator account costs one payment of USD $10, which makes it affordable for all.

There are other products out there that allow you to have online slide shows, like Slide Share (www.slideshare.com), but these may not have the rich feature set of VoiceThread.

Why Do You Use VoiceThread?

Allison has just returned from a great holiday in Mexico. Using her Flickr account (see Chapter 10), she has shared the images from her digital camera with her friends and family. All of them have commented on how exciting the trip was and what beautiful scenery there was. They all want to know more than what they can see in the pictures.

Allison loves telling people about the special significance of the different pictures and where they were taken, but she finds that often she is repeating the same stories and adventures time and time again.

Allison turns to VoiceThread. Once she opens a free basic-level account, she links her VoiceThread account to her Flickr pictures and also uploads some pictures from her computer and digital camera. She then starts to tell the story of her adventures in Mexico. She links the pictures together in a logical sequence and using a combination of text to act as captions and her own voice recorded as narration, she produces a multimedia podcast.

She shares the URL with her friends around the world as well as the new ones she made in Mexico, and they all are able to experience her Mexican adventure.

How Do You Use VoiceThread Personally?

The first step to take in making a slide show is to go to the web site and create an account (see Figure 9-1). The web site's URL is http://VoiceThread.com.

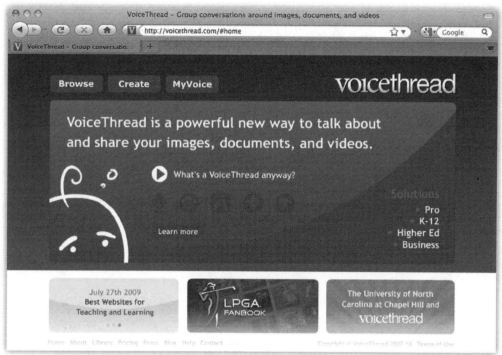

Figure 9-1 *VoiceThread home page*

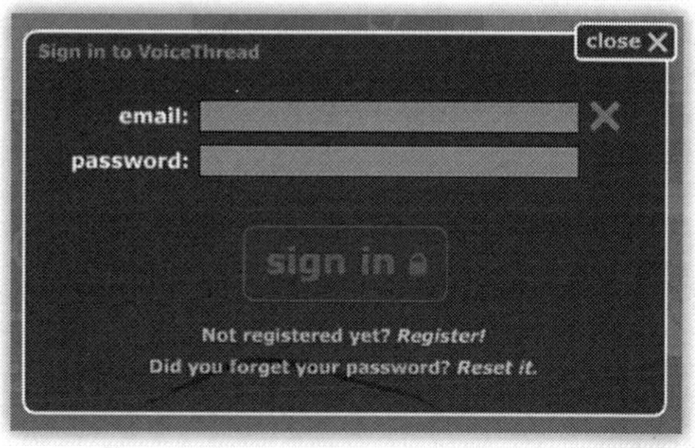

Once the web site is loaded, you need to create an account. You will do this by clicking on Create and then selecting Register (see Figure 9-2).

This then takes you to the registration process. The process is straightforward and requires a minimum amount of information (see Figure 9-3).

Figure 9-2 *Sign-in screen*

VoiceThread will ask you to create a suitable online name. It is important to consider the message you are sending in the name you choose (see appendix). You will be asked to enter a valid email address, which is needed to validate the account. You will also be asked to create a suitable password.

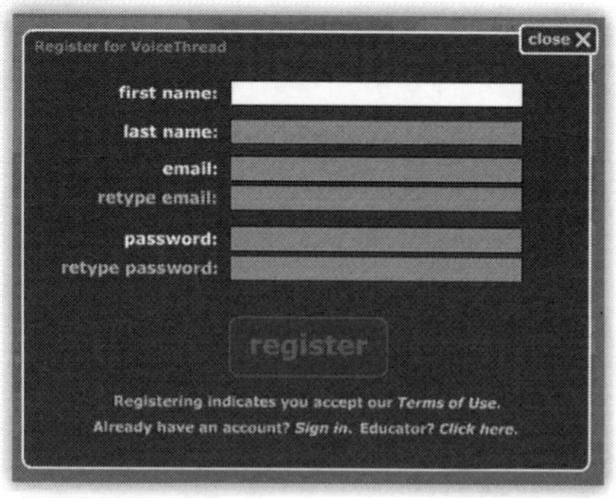

Figure 9-3 *Registration*

What Is a Suitable Password?

Almost every service we have discussed throughout this book requires a suitable password. So what is a suitable password? It's a password that should not be easy for others to guess. In general, it is recommended that your password should follow these guidelines:

- be a minimum of six characters long
- have numbers and letters
- have uppercase and lowercase letters
- contain special characters.

Also, make sure to write it down somewhere safe.

Once you have created your account, you can start making a voice thread. You can also add extra information or customize the settings of your account by clicking on the drop-down menu beside your email address in the top right-hand corner of the screen (see Figure 9-4).

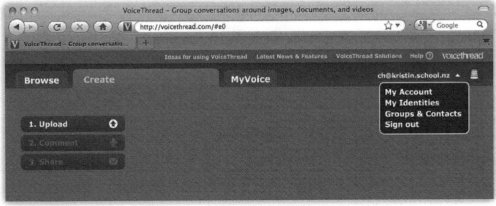

Figure 9-4 *Manage your account*

In My Account, you can upgrade to a paid account:

- change your email address and password
- add a picture of yourself to use with your comments
- purchase credits that will allow you to export your VoiceThreads

In My Identities, you can switch between your VoiceThread accounts (if you have several). This means you may have a personal account and a professional account with different viewing rights for each.

To start creating a VoiceThread, you will start by going to the Create tab and selecting Upload (see Figure 9-5). The Browse tab allows you to view presentations and the MyVoice tab is your library of VoiceThreads.

Figure 9-5 *Create tab*

In the Upload option (see Figure 9-6), you will be able to select images from your computer. You can choose images from your existing VoiceThreads or from online sources such as Flickr (see Chapter 10), Facebook (see Chapter 8), the New York Public Library, or other web sites (see Figure 9-7).

Figure 9-6 *Upload options*

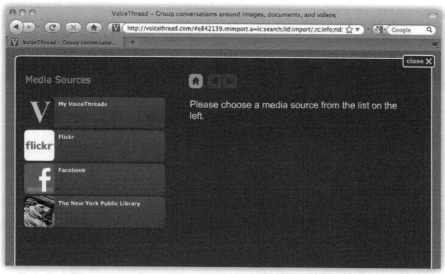

Figure 9-7 *Media sources window*

The next step is to select the images you want to use. In Figure 9-8, I am selecting images from My Computer to upload.

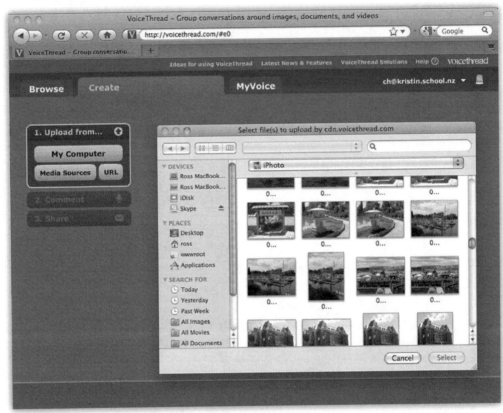

Figure 9-8 *Selecting images from My Computer*

I select a number of images. The ones I selected will be transferred to my VoiceThread account (see Figure 9-9). The speed of the upload will depend on the size of the images (bigger is slower) and the speed of the Internet connection you are using.

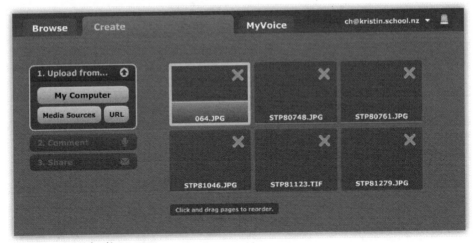

Figure 9-9 *Upload in progress*

The uploaded images are displayed as a thumbnail (see Figure 9-10). The progress of the upload is represented by a light gray bar that shows the amount that has been uploaded for each file.

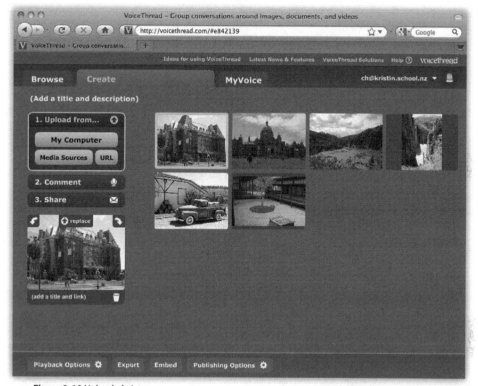

Figure 9-10 Uploaded pictures

Once the images are uploaded, you can add a title to each picture by selecting the image and then clicking on Add a title and link (see Figure 9-11). Using the selection tool will enable you to:

- add a title and link
- rotate the image clockwise or counterclockwise
- delete the image
- replace the image.

Getting the Pictures in the Right Order

Once the images are uploaded and you have added your title and descriptions, you need to arrange the pictures in the correct order. This is done by dragging the image into the correct position for the sequence you require (see Figure 9-12).

Figure 9-11 Add title/link

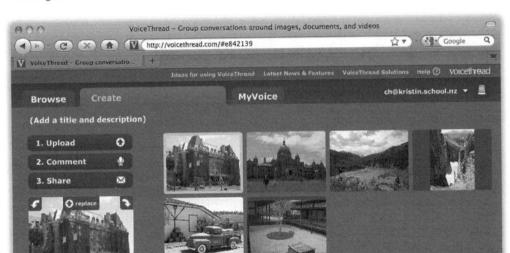

Figure 9-12 *Reorder pictures*

If you want to get images from other online accounts that you use, such as Flickr (see Chapter 10) or Facebook (see Chapter 8), click on the Media sources button to select your image source.

Adding Voice

Click on Comment (see Figure 9-13). The comments you add can be voice or text comments. Clicking the Comment button will expand the options (see Figure 9-14).

Figure 9-13 *Add comment*

Figure 9-14 *Add comment options*

Once you have expanded the Comment button, you can select what type of comment you would like to add:

- you can type in a text-based comment

- you can make a recording using the microphone on your computer for a spoken comment

- you can record a video comment using your webcam

- you can also add a comment from a telephone or uploaded from an audio file.

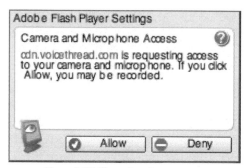

Figure 9-15 *Allow microphone use*

Click on Record to add a voice comment. The first time you use VoiceThread, your computer may ask you to allow the web browser to use your microphone (see Figure 9-15). You will need to agree to this. Click on Allow if you want to add some voice comments using your microphone.

The progress bar at the bottom will indicate how long the comment is. You can stop recording by clicking Stop recording (see Figure 9-16). You will then be asked to save or cancel your comment to this slide (see Figure 9-17).

Once you have added your voice comment, a picture representing you will appear on the left-hand side of the main picture (this is either a default avatar for you or the profile picture you have uploaded).

Figure 9-16 *Recording comment*

You can also add text-based comments to the same slide.

Now navigate either forward or backward through your slides using the arrows, adding your text or spoken comments to each slide.

Figure 9-17 *Save/delete option*

Sharing Your VoiceThread

You have a couple of things to do before you can share. You need to set the publishing options for this slide show.

Click on Publishing Properties to set the access rights to your show (see Figure 9-18). Then set the Playback options to how you would like your slide show to appear (see Figure 9-19).

Figure 9-18 *Publishing options*

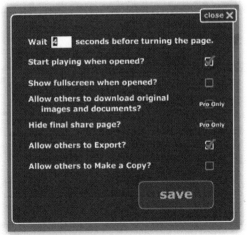

Figure 9-19 *Playback options*

You can select the options by checking or unchecking the boxes. Make sure to press Save to keep your specifications. Next, click on the Add button in the My Contacts to add an email address and save it to your Contacts (see Figures 9-20 and 9-21).

Once an email address has been added, you can email your presentation's link to your friends, family, and colleagues.

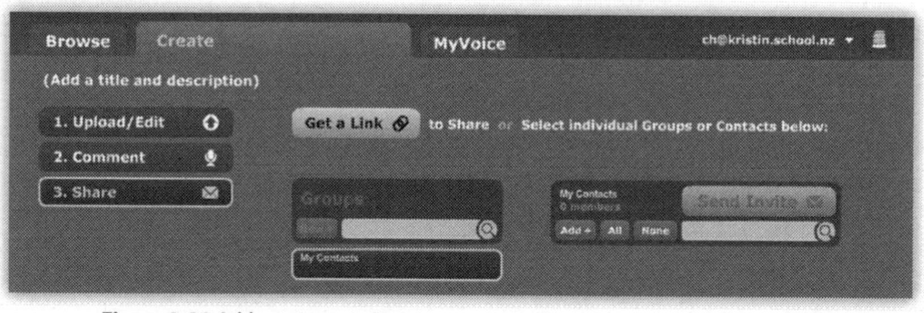

Figure 9-20 *Add contacts options*

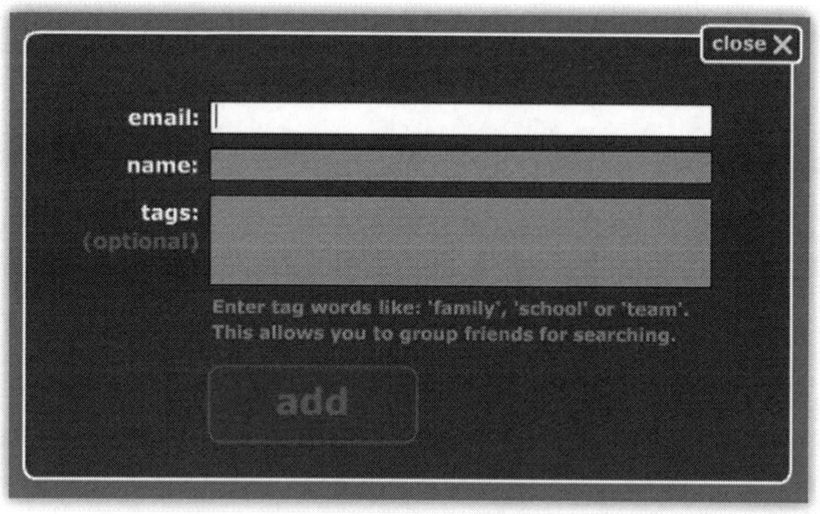

Figure 9-21 *Add email information*

Advanced Uses

This is a basic tutorial about VoiceThread, but there are many other things you can try. The following is a list of some of the ones you may find interesting:

- The Doodler—This is a simple pen tool that allows you to write or draw on your show as you are adding your comments.

- Upload video and add to your VoiceThreads.

- Use the Zoom option to zoom in on images and examine different parts.

- Export your VoiceThreads. Leave comments on friend's VoiceThread using the text, voice, and webcam options.

- Embed a VoiceThread into your blog (see Chapter 7).

How Do You Use It in a Classroom?

For Matt, the worst classroom experience he has is standing in front of his peers presenting and reporting. Faced with an audience of his classmates, his throat dries up, his voice crackles and stutters, and he flushes a brilliant red color. Matt's research is meticulous and his content excellent, but his best laid plans and notes make little sense when faced with the attention of his friends. He fumbles his way through his presentation.

Michael, his classmate, is the opposite. He speaks with a clear and articulate manner, his voice is animated and alive and he is confident. His work is of a high standard and worth seeing not once but several times.

Andrea, their humanities teacher, regularly has the students present their research and curriculum to the class. Andrea knows from Dale's Learning Cone that by both teaching and presenting material to the class, she will have the best retention of knowledge. She is faced with a dilemma. The material they are presenting represents a portion of the curriculum and the students need to be able to study this content for the examinations. She is also acutely aware of Matt's shyness.

To deal with the repeatability aspect, to help Matt share his excellent knowledge and content, and to utilize Michael's charismatic presentations, Andrea turns to VoiceThread.

The teaching process is the same. The students define the problem and do their secondary research. Once they have completed this aspect, some of them undertake primary research. They then design a solution, laying out how they are going to structure their presentation, creating a mind map using Mindmeister, and preparing their presenters' notes.

The students then develop their slides either directly in VoiceThread or in a presentation tool and upload it to VoiceThread. Once the slides are added, the students then narrate their presentation.

For Matt, the absence of an audience means his speech is more articulate and flowing, and he conveys the message and content of the presentation without embarrassment or discomfort. For Michael, he is able to present his content with his usual flair and record this as an excellent exemplar for future student use. His peers leave voice comments on his VoiceThread saying how good his presentation was and how much they enjoyed it. Matt's sense of humor, previously lost in the stress of the spotlight, comes to the forefront.

For Andrea, the students' collection of VoiceThreads provides an excellent learning resource for her class. They become a core element of the e-portfolio she is preparing for each of her students. Her students are more engaged, and Matt has shown the quality of his research and preparation in his final presentation.

The class is able to access the VoiceThreads at any time, and this makes their preparation for examinations and assessment easier, rather than relying on memory.

Classroom Examples That Cultivate The 21st Century Fluencies

- **Solution Fluency**—Students can link and integrate many different aspects of communications including voice, images, video, and text in to a single product. *Examples:* Students in the French Language class use VoiceThread to create a presentation as the solution to a project investigating Paris and its environment; prepare the script in English and add subtitles, but use the voice recording feature to record the narration in French.

- **Information Fluency**—Students can broadcast information in a variety of modes that address the learning styles of the visual, auditory, and read/write learners. *Example:* Collate information about a mathematics concept from a variety of sources and then present the collated and processed information in a VoiceThread presentation.

- **Collaboration Fluency**—Students can add a personal aspect to the feedback and comment process by commenting on the VoiceThread in both text and voice form. *Examples:* Investigate a current social studies issue and report using VoiceThread; view peers' work and leave suitable critique and comment, using text and voice comments.

- **Creativity Fluency**—VoiceThread allows the developer to use a wide range of media in a straightforward linear development tool. The focus is on the product rather than the tool. *Example:* English students are asked to prepare a static image based on a contemporary piece of poetry. The students present each verse as a spoken narration and written caption. The students suitably source, request permission, and cite the static images that form the main focus of presentation.

- **Media Fluency**—Students can link and sequence commentary, images, video, and captioning to develop a product that is efficient, logical, and end-user friendly. *Examples:* The students in English class are asked to storyboard a video they will produce. The students use digital cameras to create establishing shots. They import these into VoiceThread. The students sequence the images and add script as a spoken narration and add movement action and camera angles as captions. This produces a digital storyboard with realistic timing.

Summary

- In this chapter, you opened a VoiceThread account. Then you uploaded images to the account from your computer or accessed ones that are in your Facebook or Flickr account. You can also use images that you have located on the Web by adding the web address using the URL link.

- With your images uploaded, you arranged them into the correct sequence and added titles, links, voice comments, and text comments. Having completed this, you set the publishing and playback options and shared the link to the slide show with your friends.

- VoiceThread has brought your pictures to life. You have been able to not only share your pictures with your contacts, but also explain in your own words the significance of each image.

Questions to Ask

- Should I make my slide shows public or private?

- Whom should I invite to see my slides?

- Should I moderate comments people leave on the VoiceThreads?

- Am I allowed to use the images I have included in my VoiceThread? Are they protected by copyright?

- Should I allow people to download my images and content? Can they export or download my slide show?

Resources

Starter sheet on VoiceThread—http://edorigami.wikispaces.com/Starter+Sheets

A VoiceThread tutorial—http://VoiceThread.com/share/558435

VoiceThread help—http://VoiceThread.com/help/faq

VoiceThread instruction manuals—http://VoiceThread.com/help/manuals

VoiceThread tutorials using VoiceThread—http://VoiceThread.com/?#c28

Video Tutorials on VoiceThread Introduction—
http://eduwrite.blogspot.com/2008/09/VoiceThread-tutorial.htm

Chapter 10
Media Sharing

> Of all of our inventions for mass communication, pictures still speak the most universally understood language.
>
> **Walt Disney**

Expectations: What Will You Learn?

In this chapter, you will share your favorite images, graphics , and even videos using the online photo-sharing web site Flickr. You will work through the process of creating an account, uploading pictures, setting tags and descriptions, sharing these with your friends, and managing your privacy. You will have the opportunity to explore Flickr and see some of the best photography in the world.

Media Sharing Terminology

Download refers to taking files such as photographs or video from a web site and saving them to a computer or some other type of digital device.

File formats are the styles or types of image files that software such as Flickr will be able to read and display. The most common file format that we will use is the .JPG image format.

Flickr is the media sharing web site located at www.flickr.com.

JPG is an abbreviation for Joint Photographic Experts Group. JPG (pronounced jay-peg) is the most common image file format and most cameras and scanners will save pictures into this format.

MB is an abbreviation for megabyte, which is a measure of the size of a file. A megabyte is 1024 KB, or kilobytes, of data. 1024 MB of data makes a gigabyte or GB.

Photostream is a term used to describe the pictures uploaded by a user.

Pixels are dots of a single color within an image. Most images are several megapixels, which means the image is made up of several million dots. An image that is 1024 pixels wide by 768 pixels high (this is the size of the average computer screen) is about ¾ of a megabyte or 750 kilobytes in size.

Sets refers to a group of related images. Using these collections, or sets, makes organizing images into themes or categories simple and manageable.

Upload means taking a file such as a picture or video and sending it to your Flickr account.

What Is Flickr?

Flickr is one of several photo-sharing sites. Most sights have similar features that allow you to:

- create an account that can be private (only viewable by the owner of the account and invited friends/family) or public (viewable by anyone)
- upload pictures and, in some cases, video
- add tags and descriptions to the pictures
- comment on images.

Flickr is one of the most popular sites with more than 3 billion images uploaded to it by its members. Some of the other photo-sharing sites are:

- Photobucket (see Figure 10-1)—http://photobucket.com

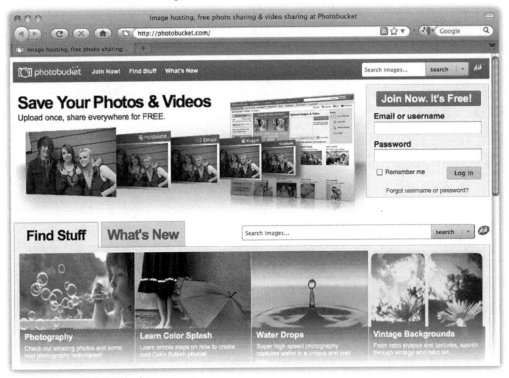

Figure 10-1 *Photobucket*

● Webshots (see Figure 10-2)—http://webshots.com

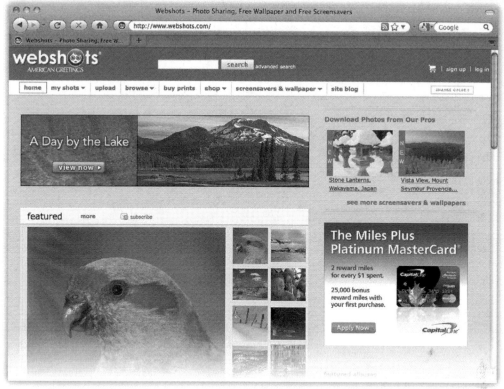

Figure 10-2 *Webshots*

Most of these sites have free memberships that include basic functions. For more advanced features and greater monthly uploads, you could purchase a premium membership. Flickr allows you to upload 100 MB of images and two videos (of up to 100 MB in size) to your account per month.

What is 100 MB?

MB is an abbreviation for megabyte. A megabyte is a measure of the size of a file. An image of medium quality is approximately 1 MB in size. Usually the bigger the file size, the better the quality of the image.

Why Did We Select Flickr?

Flickr is an easy-to-use tool with a good starting package available to all at no cost. Flickr's basic account gives you 100 MB of uploads per month, which is about 100 good-quality images (about three megapixels each). It also allows you to upload video clips.

Flickr gives you a degree of control over who can see your images and also allows you to set different levels of copyright control over the pictures. Other online tools, such as VoiceThread (see Chapter 9) and Facebook (see Chapter 8) link to Flickr as a source of your images.

What is a megapixel? Mega means million, and pixels are the dots that make up an image. The more pixels or dots there are in an image, the higher the quality of the image and the larger you can print it without seeing the pixels (seeing the pixels or dots in an image is called pixilation). It is important to remember the GIGO rule. No matter how many pixels you have in your image, and some cameras are now 18 or even 25 megapixels, if the picture is poor, it's just a big bad picture. GIGO is an abbreviation for Garbage In = Garbage Out.

Why Do You Use a Photo-Sharing Site?

Catherine's son Brendan, his wife, and their children have recently moved to the United Kingdom. While they are talking every day using Skype (see Chapter 5), Catherine wants to have pictures that she can share with her friends. Skype allows the family to stay in touch, but with the time zone differences and the distance, it's not always easy to share pictures with her friends.

Brendan has a solution. He opens an account on the photo-sharing web site Flickr. He uploads the pictures he has taken of the family on his digital camera to the web site and invites Catherine, the children's grandmother, to share the pictures. Catherine creates an account and follows Brendan's photostream. Brendan regularly updates his pictures on the photostream so Catherine is able to show her friends the latest pictures of her family.

Catherine also downloads some images and takes these to the local mall, where she prints them out at a photo kiosk. Sometimes she even orders photos online, from a service that is provided by Flickr.

Soon Catherine has purchased her own digital camera and is uploading images of herself and her friends for her family in the United Kingdom to view, share, and print. Catherine discovers by accident that her new digital camera has a video recording function and starts uploading short video clips and messages to Flickr as well.

Flickr, the online photo-sharing web site, has enabled Catherine and her family to stay in touch.

How Do You Use Flickr Personally?

The first step is to create an account on Flickr. To do this, you are going to need a Yahoo! ID. By way of explanation, Yahoo! owns Flickr. If you already have a Yahoo! ID, you can jump straight into opening an account. If you don't, you'll start the same way but add one extra step in order to create a Yahoo! ID.

First, open your web browser and go to www.flickr.com (see Figure 10-3).

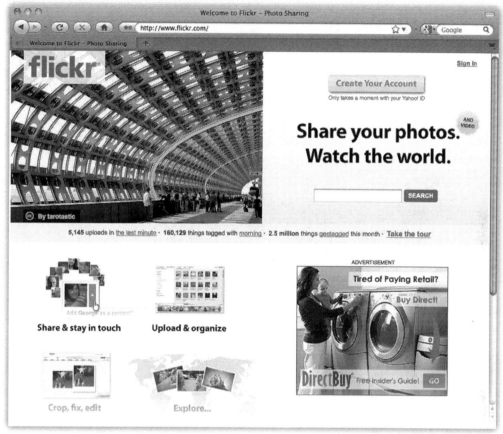

Figure 10-3 *Flickr home page*

Now click on the Create Your Account button. This will start the account creation process. If you have a Yahoo! ID, you can now sign in. If you don't, click on the Sign Up link at the bottom of the page. This will allow you to create a Yahoo! ID (see Figure 10-4).

Sign in to Yahoo!

Are you protected?
Create your sign-in seal.
(Why?)

Yahoo! ID:

(e.g. free2rhyme@yahoo.com)

Password:

☑ **Keep me signed in**
for 2 weeks unless I sign out. info
[Uncheck if on a shared computer]

Sign In

I can't access my account | Help

Don't have a Yahoo! ID?
Signing up is easy.
Sign Up

What Is a Yahoo! ID?

Essentially, a Yahoo! ID is a membership to all of the Yahoo! tools and services. It's a free and simple process. Microsoft has a similar tool called the MSN Passport.

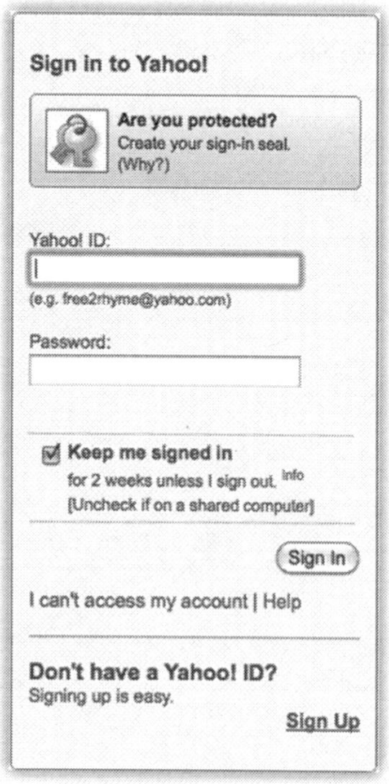

Figure 10-4 *Yahoo! sign in*

Creating a Yahoo! ID

The process of getting a Yahoo! ID is easy. You enter the information in the indicated fields (see Figure 10-5). In the second part, Select an ID and password, you can check the availability of your preferred name. It is always important to consider what message you are sending when you select an online ID. Is it professional and appropriate? What would an employer who saw this think?

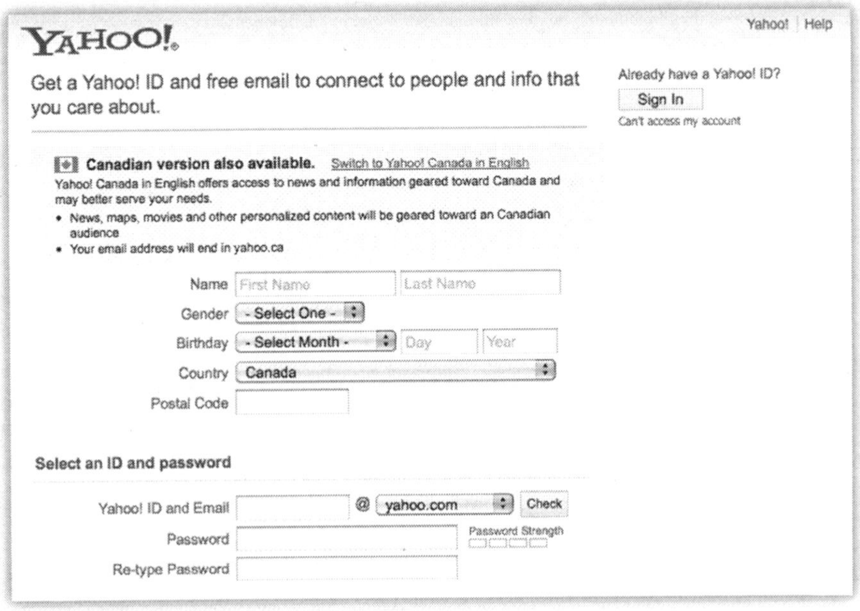

Figure 10-5 *Create Yahoo! ID*

Like almost all sign-up pages, you will be asked to copy a code into the field to prove you are a person rather than a computer (see Figure 10-6). The Yahoo! ID check system is case sensitive, so you have to include capital and small letters as they appear in the code. Once you have created your account, you will receive an email to confirm your registration and finalize the process. The email will have a link you will need to click to confirm the account.

Figure 10-6 *Yahoo! ID check system*

The next step is to log in to your account using your Yahoo! ID and password. You have created your Yahoo! ID and started your Flickr account. You now need to customize your Flickr account and upload some pictures. When you sign in (see Figure 10-7), you will be asked to give your Flickr account a name. I have used the name of my Yahoo! ID, but you are free to choose any name you like.

Figure 10-7 Create Flickr name

Click on Create a New Account. Now, all that's left to do is customize the account, upload your pictures, and share them with your friends or even the world (see Figure 10-8)!

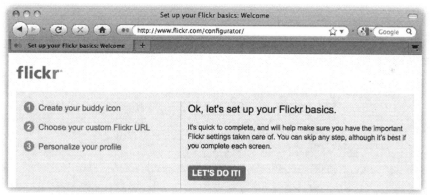

Figure 10-8 Getting started

Click on Personalize your profile and enter a bit of information. Much of the information requested is optional; add it only if you want. Next, choose a web address or URL. In Figure 10-9, I have chosen to use my Yahoo! ID as my custom Flickr URL. The URL I will give to my friends and family to access my pictures is www.flickr.com/photos/thedigitaldiet.

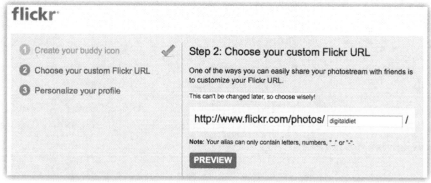

Figure 10-9 Choose URL

The last step in personalizing your profile is adding information as shown in Figure 10-10. If you like, you can skip this part because none of the information is required.

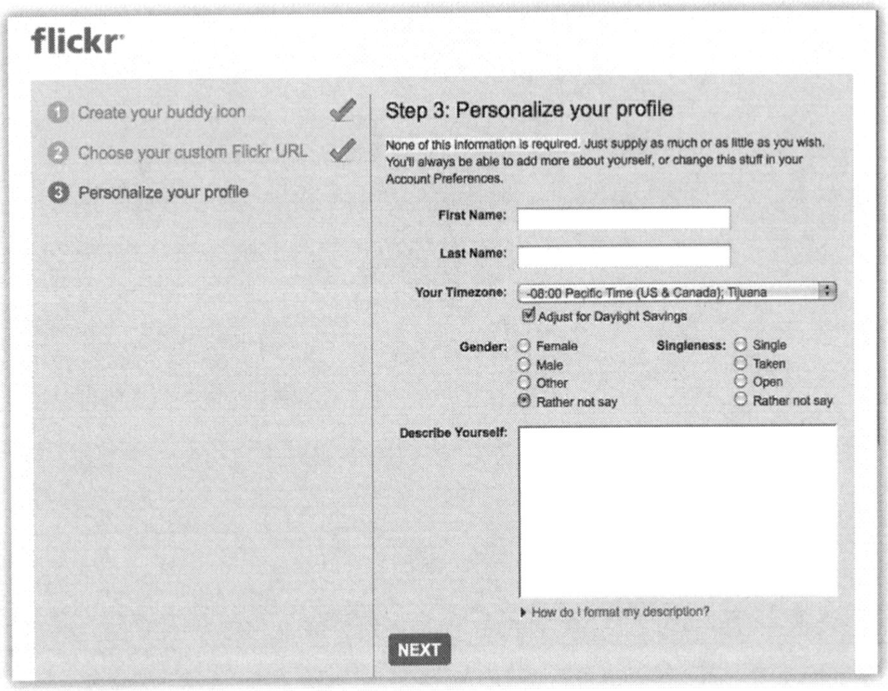

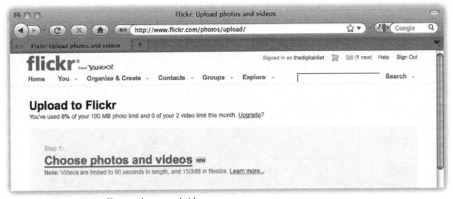

Figure 10-10 *Personalize profile*

Now that you've accessed your free Flickr account, you can upload up to 100 MB of pictures to the account, which is about 100 good-quality pictures. To do this, you need to have the pictures stored on your computer, a CD or DVD, or even a memory card.

Figure 10-11 *Choose photos and videos*

Click on Choose photos and videos (see Figure 10-11). This will open an explorer window on your computer that allows you to select your pictures from your computer, CD, DVD, or a memory card (see Figure 10-12).

Figure 10-12 *Open after selecting images*

Once you have selected your images, click on Open in the lower right-hand corner of the window. This will bring you to a confirmation screen. Here you can set the level of privacy you would like on your images (see Figure 10-13). You can make them public, so that anyone can see them, or you can make them private and allow only your friends to see them.

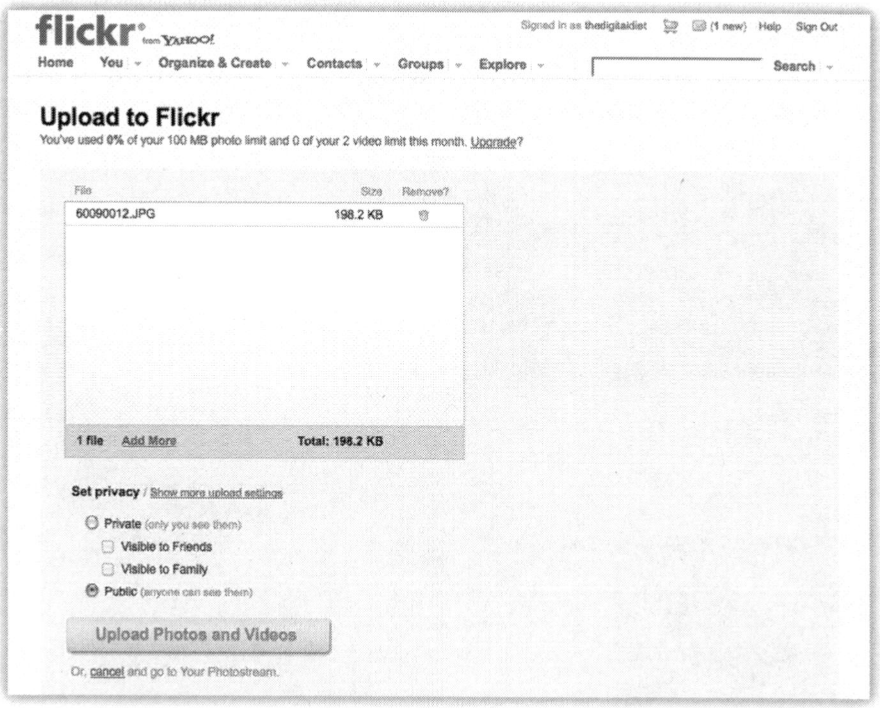

Figure 10-13 *Set privacy*

Clicking on Upload Photos and Videos will start the uploading of your pictures. The time it will take to upload the files will depend on the following factors:

- how big the files are
- how many files you are uploading
- the speed of your Internet connection
- how many people are using Flickr at the time you are using it.

This part of the process can sometimes be very quick and other times quite a bit slower.

Tags, Title, and Descriptions

When you have uploaded your pictures, you will be asked to add tags, titles, and descriptions to your images (see Figure 10-14).

- Tags are keywords that can be used to search for pictures. The ones I used in Figure 10-14 are Animals, Zoo, Memphis, and 2009. These pictures were taken during a visit to the Memphis Zoo in 2009.
- Titles are helpful—if you add a descriptive title, you can tell at a glance what the picture or video is about.
- Descriptions allow you to tell the story behind the picture and set the scene. They are terrific for explaining the background to the great family picture or the sweeping cityscape you snapped on a trip.

Figure 10-14 *Add tags, titles, and descriptions*

Getting Organized

Just uploading your pictures into Flickr works when you only have a few pictures, but as you add more pictures you will need to get organized by adding some structure.

You can do this by creating Sets (see Figure 10-15). Sets are collections or folders of similar or related photos and videos.

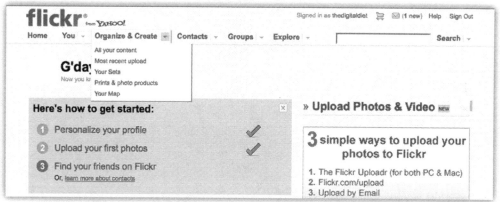

Figure 10-15 *Choosing sets from drop-down menu*

To organize and keep my pictures from the trip to Memphis Zoo together, I want to create a set called Memphis Zoo 2009. I click on the Sets tab (see Figure 10-16) and create a new set.

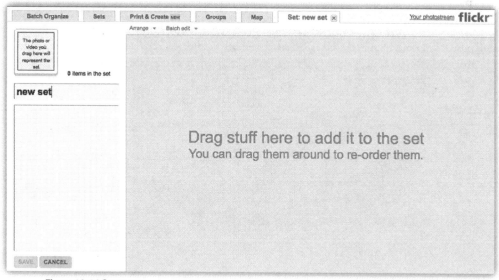

Figure 10-16 *Create sets*

Once you create a title and add a description, you can drag one of the pictures into the picture frame above the title and description to represent this set, much like a title page or a book cover. Then you drag the rest of the pictures from the content pane at the bottom into this new set (see Figure 10-17).

Figure 10-17 *Add pictures*

When you have added all the pictures you want to the set, click on Save. If at some later date you want to add more pictures, you simply open the set and drag the pictures from the Content pane into the set. Deleting or removing them from a set is as simple as selecting the image and dragging it out of the pane. Figure 10-18 shows what my finished set looks like.

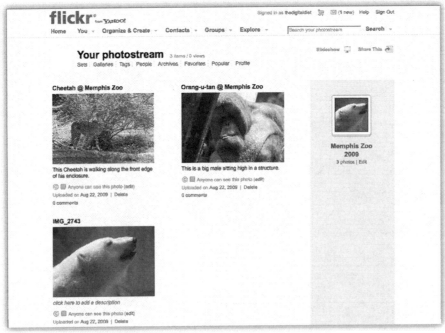

Figure 10-18 *Finished set*

Advanced Uses

The following are some techniques or tips to stretch the advanced user:

- Adapt and modify your pictures using iPhoto for Mac, FotoSketcher for PC (www.fotosketcher.com), or online tools such as PhotoFunia (www.photofunia.com) or Google's Picasa (picasa.google.com)

- Use your Flickr images in your VoiceThreads and arrange a feed to your social networking account on Facebook.

- Set up a class Flickr account and restrict the access so only your students can use it.

- Share video using Flickr. Upload and share your video creations with your friends or class.

Flickr isn't alone; there are many other media-sharing sites, including the hugely popular YouTube. Users who find the video sharing on Flickr to be limited can create a YouTube (www.youtube.com) or TeacherTube (www.teachertube.com) account. You can upload and share your creations using these tools.

How Do I Use It in a Classroom?

Allanah's fourth-grade class went to the zoo as part of a conservation unit they were studying. The students knew they had to create a short story about the trip using VoiceThread (see Chapter 9) and focus on one animal they had seen at the zoo.

The students had three digital cameras to use to take pictures of the animals and the zoo. These would be used as the basis of their multimedia creations.

The students had a great time at the zoo, the cameras were passed around, and each student had the opportunity to take pictures. Several of the students brought their own cameras along as well.

When they returned to school, the images were downloaded onto the class computer and the students were asked to pick their best three images to share. The selected images were then checked by the teacher and uploaded to the class Flickr account. The students were reminded how to access the images, and they had to check out their pictures for homework.

The students then worked through the development process for creating and publishing their multimedia short story. They followed four easy steps, the 4Ds problem-solving process of which Solution Fluency is comprised. They were first introduced by Ted McCain in Teaching for Tomorrow.

- **Define**—The students defined and understood their task. The teacher outlined the range of themes they were allowed to cover and the parameters for how many slides and how long their story was to be. (Much of this was done before the students went on the field trip.) The students were told how they would be assessed and were provided with a clear statement of expectations.

- **Design**—The students developed the story they wanted to share with the class. They used a mind-mapping tool (a very good online tool is at www.mindmeister.com) to storyboard their production. They sequenced the images they were going to use and the captions they wanted to include and developed an image-by-image script. The teacher and the students individually discussed their designs as they worked through the design process. The teacher reminded the students of the two key design questions:

  - *Is it suitable for the audience?*

  - *Is it suitable for the purpose?*

  The teacher was able to provide feedback on the designs as she worked with the student and looked at the images they had selected on Flickr.

- **Do**—The students created their VoiceThread (see Chapter 9) and used the images in the class Flickr account to provide captivating visuals for the story. The teacher and the students individually discussed their VoiceThreads as they developed them, and the teacher was able to provide feedback on the VoiceThreads and the quality of the product.

- **Debrief**—Allanah asked the students to do a self-evaluation of the process they had undertaken and the product they produced. Since she had given the students the assessment criteria at the start of the task, the students used these rubrics to do a self-assessment. This was an excellent starting point for Allanah to provide formative assessment that the students could use to develop and improve on.

Classroom Examples That Cultivate The 21st Century Fluencies

- **Solution Fluency**—Students can use a hosting site as the end point of developing a solution—publishing the product. *Example:* Students studying Media Studies produce a video as the culmination of their course. They work through the process of Defining the problem, Designing the solution, and Developing the solution. The last part of the development phase is to publish their completed video.

- **Information Fluency**—Students have the opportunity to use keywords and descriptions to make their images and video more accessible and search friendly. *Examples:* students in Grade 7 visited the local zoo. Each group of students had a digital camera and documented the animals they saw. The students then shared the images using the class Flickr account. The students had to provide suitable keywords to describe the images and within the description field provide a brief summary of the material detailed in the image. The other students are able to quickly and easily locate the images using keywords their peers entered.

- **Collaboration Fluency**—Students can use interest groups, with moderated discussion forums and image publishing to collaborate on areas of interest and passion. *Example:* The students in the previous example use Flickr to collaborate, edit the keywords and descriptions to ensure they have the most accurate information. They also collaborate by uploading and sharing their images and video clips.

- **Creativity Fluency**—Students can use a publishing medium and discussion forum as an outlet for the creative talents. The comments and favorites features allows feedback and critique. *Examples:* Students in Grade 12 Art are working in a digital medium using various graphical development tools by constructing and editing imagery. The students upload their evolutions as they develop the final product and invite their peers to offer critiques. Flickr became their publishing medium.

- **Media Fluency**—Students can publish and organize their media into groups and sets based on the theme, genre, or content of their images and videos. *Examples:* The Grade 11 Photography students use the creative commons search criteria to find images they are able to use under a creative commons license. The students then refine their search criteria to locate specific images that relate to genre and style of photography they are studying. The students are using an ethical approach to locating and using images.

Summary

- In this chapter, you looked at why you would use a photo sharing site like Flickr and walked through the process of opening a Flickr account.

- You customized your Flickr account and selected a suitable name.

- You were also able to customize a URL or web address to share with your friends and family, which you can email to them so they can view your pictures.

- Finally, you uploaded some pictures to your account and added titles, tags, and descriptions to make the pictures easy to search for, with explanations of what they are about. Then you organized these pictures into a set based on a theme or an event.

Questions to Ask

- Who is going to see these pictures and videos? What should I set the privacy level at?

- Is this an appropriate picture to upload?

- Is it suitable?

- Is it OK for me to share this photograph or video? Have I asked the other people who are in this media?

- Is this material protected by copyright?

Resources

Tutorials series on Flickr—
www.indezine.com/mediamazine/2006/05/flickr-tutorials-series.html

FlickrBits Tutorials on Flickr—www.flickrbits.com/docs

Flickr Tutorials on video—www.flickrbits.com/docs

www.youtube.com/watch?v=Re05530ulS4&feature=related

Newbie's Guide to Flickr—http://news.cnet.com/8301-17939_109-9703620-2.html

An extensive list of posts on Recipester—
www.recipester.org/Topics/Flickr?by=recent&time=all

Classroom uses for Flickr—
http://web20-instruction.wikispaces.com/Using+Flickr+for+Instruction

Google Picasa—http://picasa.google.com

Apple iPhoto—http://www.apple.com/iphoto

PhotoFunia—http://www.photofunia.com

FotoSketcher—http://www.fotosketcher.com/

Appendix
Email

Email allows you to quickly and easily send messages to thousands of people all around the world—even those who really don't care what you have to say.

Ian Jukes

Expectations: What Will You Learn?

One of the foundational tools of the World Wide Web is electronic mail, or email. Whether you are using it to communicate with your friends, to send attachments like files or pictures, or to validate your access to a new Internet service, email is a fundamental tool to use.

In this chapter, you will look at signing up with a free online email provider and will walk through the basics of sending emails, replying to them, attaching files, and adding signatures to your messages.

Email Terminology

Attachment is a file or image that has been attached to the email message.

BCC is an abbreviation for blind carbon copy. This is a hidden recipient of the message you are sending. People receiving this message will not be able to see anyone who has been included in the BCC field.

Body is the main part of the message where you add your text. It is equivalent to the written letter in a conventional mail system.

CC stands for carbon copy. This is the field in the email message where you can enter addresses for secondary recipients.

Client-based email is where you have a client or program installed on your computer that connects to the online email server. The client downloads the messages and stores them on your computer and uploads messages you are sending to the email server. Using a client allows you to always have access to your messages but only on the computer your have installed the client on. Again, you need to be online to send and receive messages, but you can construct messages offline.

Email is the abbreviation of electronic mail. Email can be as simple as only text or more sophisticated messages contain images, video, or attached files.

Gmail is a free web-based email service provided by Google. We will examine Gmail in this appendix.

Head is the part of the email message that contains the address of the recipients, the subject line, and attachments. This is the equivalent of the envelope in a conventional letter.

Hotmail is a free web-based email service provided by Microsoft. You will need to create a Windows Live ID to set up a Hotmail account.

Server is the computer that collects and sends out your email messages. The server routes the messages you send via a series of steps to the server that is hosting the message recipient's email account and from there to the message recipient.

Signature is a text element that is added to the email message, usually containing the email author's contact details. This is automatically added to the end of most email messages.

Subject is the field where you indicate what the message is about. It is considered bad manners to not have a subject line in an email message. Subject lines make it easier to manage messages and quickly sort through them.

To: is the key address field where you put the email address of the primary recipient of the message. You must have a primary recipient in an email message.

Web-based email is an email account where the messages are stored on the email server on the Internet, such as Hotmail and gmail. These messages can be accessed anywhere you have Internet access. However, if you do not have Internet access, you cannot gain access to your messages.

What Is Email?

Email is an abbreviation for electronic mail. It is the electronic equivalent of a conventional letter. An email message, unlike a conventional letter, can be easily and almost instantly sent to many people, with files and images attached. With an email message, you also can ask for a "read receipt" to tell you if the message has been read by the recipients.

With a conventional letter, you need an envelope and stamp, both of which cost money. With email, the cost is reduced (you still have to pay for your Internet connection and computer). With a conventional letter, it can take a long time to reach its destination. However, with electronic mail, if your recipient is online, the message can be received almost instantly.

With conventional mail, if you want to send your letter to many people, you need to make many copies of the message and then buy lots of stamps and envelopes. With email, you just add more names to the To:, CC:, and/or BCC: fields.

Unfortunately, most people with email accounts will receive unsolicited or unrequested email messages, commonly known as spam. Spam messages often advertise products or invite recipients to visit a specific web site.

Email is fast, cheap, and easy. The messages are always easier to read than some people's handwriting and can contain files and pictures. That said, an email does not replace the pleasure of receiving a letter (unless it's a bill)—the two forms of communication can complement each other.

What's in an Email Address?

An email address will have several key elements for it to be valid. The address must have:

- a user name—this is the name of the person; for example, Anybody

- the @ symbol—this stands for at; for example, Anybody@

- the domain name of server (online computer) that hosts your email account; for example, Anybody@gmail.com (this is read: anybody at gmail dot com)

- Some email addresses also have a country code after the domain name; for example, Anybody@yahoo.co.nz (which is read: Anybody at yahoo dot com dot New Zealand).

What is in an email message? Let's have a look at the different parts of a message and then work through the process of setting up an email account and sending a message.

The Anatomy of an Email Message

Figure A-1 details the different components of an email message. An email message consists of two parts: the head, which is like the envelope a letter comes in, and the body, which is like the letter inside the envelope. The head includes the names of the recipients, the sender's name, a subject line, the date and time of sending, and the urgency of the message. Sometimes the head will have attachments, which are files added to the email message.

The body of the email message, which is like the letter in the envelope, contains all the content of the message. Often it will have a signature that the email program automatically adds to the bottom of the message. This is where you put all the detail of your message.

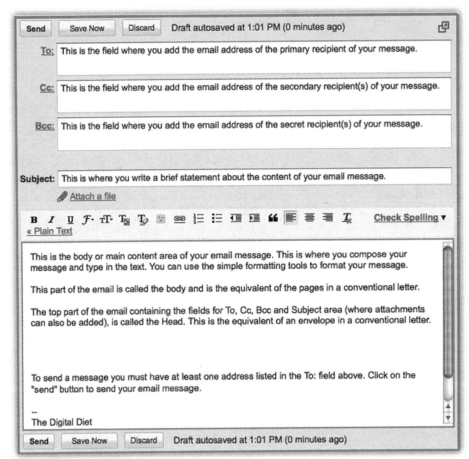

Figure A-1 *Email message*

How Do You Use Email Personally?

The uses of email range from casual communications with friends to official messages to business colleagues. For many people, email is no longer a luxury item, but rather an absolute necessity that allows them to communicate quickly and efficiently around the planet. Its speed and ability to transfer files make email indispensable in business and pleasure.

To even start to make use of the many tools available to you on the Internet, you will need an email account. Many online web services require the person signing up to have an email account so they can send emails confirming the person's account.

Which Email Service Should You Use?

In this chapter, we are going to sign up for Google's Gmail. Gmail is not the only free email service available, but it's a good place to start. Microsoft, Yahoo!, and several other companies offer similar products. We picked Gmail because it is one of the most successful and offers the most storage for the right price—nothing!

A Comparison of Popular Email Services

Product	Storage	Company	URL
Gmail	7GB	Google	www.gmail.com
Hotmail	5GB	Microsoft	www.hotmail.com
Yahoo! Mail	Unlimited	Yahoo!	www.yahoomail.com

Getting Started

Your starting place is your web browser (this could be Microsoft's Internet Explorer, Mozilla's Firefox, or Apple's Safari or Opera). Enter the web address (also called a URL) in the browser's address bar (see Figure A-2). The address for Gmail is www.gmail.com. Next, click on Create an account. This will take you through to the sign-up page (see Figure A-3).

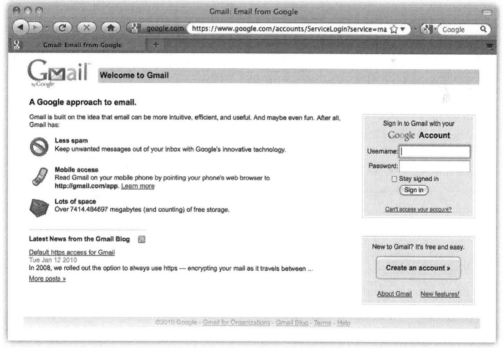

Figure A-2 *Gmail*

To start your account, you need to enter some key pieces of information. These include your first and last name and your "login" name. This is the name that will appear in your email address and that you will use to access this email account. It is important that to consider what you choose as your login name, as this may be the email address you have to use for official communications.

Figure A-3 *Sign-up page*

If you make your login name too long or unwieldy, it might affect your ability to quickly send and receive emails. You can check to see if your email address is available by clicking on the Check availability button. You will also need to enter this additional information:

- Your password should be numbers and letters, at least eight characters long, and shouldn't be too predictable.

- The Security question will help you get access to your email if you forget your password.

- Your Location is approximately where you live on the planet.

- Word verification—This is a security check to prevent computer programs from starting email accounts.

- Terms of Service—Most people skip over this part and just click on the accept button. It is always good practice to read these before accepting them.

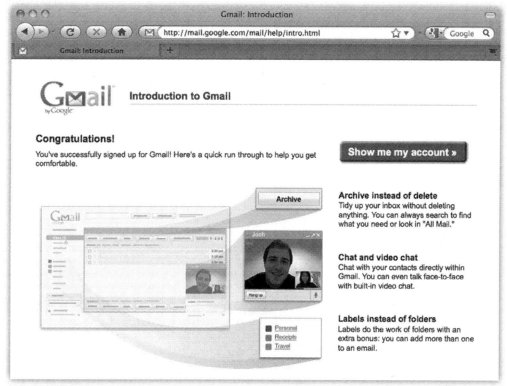

Figure A-4 *Welcome*

Once you have been through this process you will be linked to the start page (see Figure A-4). This page will give you a tour of Gmail, or you can connect directly to your email account.

Clicking on the Show me my account button opens your Gmail account (see Figure A-5). In the upper right-hand corner of the page, the link to your personal settings (the information about you), as well as your email address, is displayed. My email address is thedigitaldiet@gmail.com.

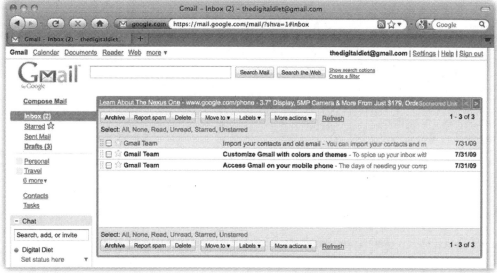

Figure A-5 *Gmail account*

While we're going to mainly focus on email here, Gmail does have a number of other features you can explore later. These features include:

- text-based chat

- voice and video chat capabilities for your computer if it has a microphone and webcam

- access to your gmail, calendars, Google documents, and a wide range of other services and tools.

On the left side of the page are your links to your Inbox, Sent items, and Draft messages (messages you are working on and have not yet sent).

Reading a Message

To read a message, just click on the header (title) and the message will open. Figure A-6 shows the first message in my mailbox, one that was sent to me by Gmail.

If I wanted to reply to this message, I would just click on the Reply button, which would open a new message to send to the original sender (see Figure A-6).

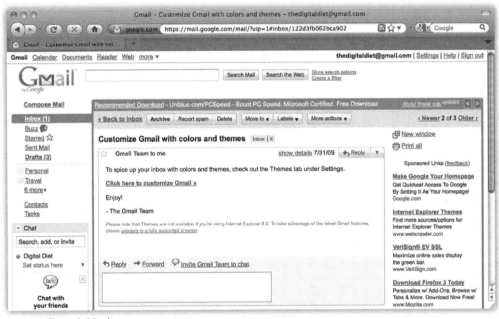

Figure A-6 *Reply*

If I wanted to send this message to someone else, I would click on the Forward link and it would be sent to the email recipient I put in the To: field.

Sending a Message

Start by clicking on the Compose Mail button (see Figure A-7). This will open a new message form for you.

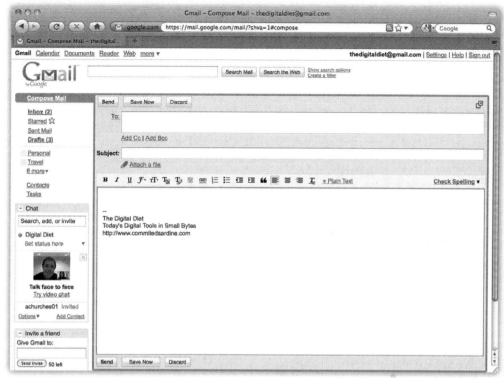

Figure A-7 *Compose mail*

The new message will load into the main pane of your Gmail page (see Figure A-8). You can add an email address in the To: field. You can also add more than one address to any of the address fields (To:, CC:, or BCC:). When the message first opens, the CC and BCC fields are not expanded. You just click on the Add CC or Add BCC links to add recipients to these fields.

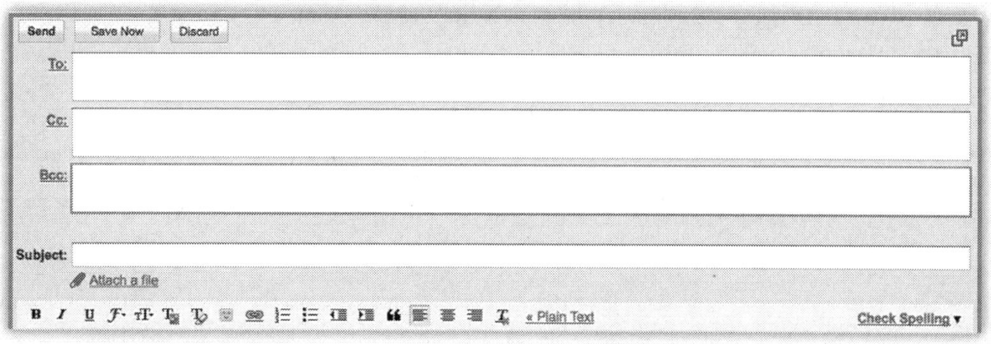

Figure A-8 *Message window*

Then add a Subject line. The subject line is a simple statement about the topic or contents of the email. A descriptive subject line makes managing and sorting your email messages much easier.

Next, enter your message in the body of the email. You can format the contents of the email message using the simple editing tools available in the Edit toolbar (see Figure A-9).

Figure A-9 *Edit toolbar*

Once you have completed the message, you just click on Send to send it to your recipients.

Adding a Signature

A signature is a small amount of text or personal information that gets added to the bottom of all of your messages. Often the signature will have your contact details. To add a signature, click on Settings in the top right-hand corner of the Gmail window. The Settings button is just to the right of your email address on the right side of the screen.

In the Signature section, add your personal information (see Figure A-10). Make sure you have clicked in the radio button that switches between No signature and the box that contains your signature. Then scroll to the bottom of the page to save your changes.

Figure A-10 *Signature*

A good idea that is to limit the amount of information contained in your signature to an email address, web site, or perhaps a phone number. It's not such a good idea to include your address for reasons of safety and security.

The Setting page also allows you adjust your Gmail account. This includes setting up a video chat, adding a picture of yourself, and adding email contacts from another email account.

Adding Contacts

The last part of this appendix is about adding your contacts. Contacts are the all people and organizations you want to regularly send your emails to. As you receive emails, you can add these new email addresses to your contacts list or you can enter them by clicking on the Contacts link. This opens the Contacts pane in the Gmail window (see Figure A-11).

Figure A-11 *Contacts*

Then click on the Add contacts icon in the top left-hand corner of the Contacts pane. This opens the Contact information sheet and you can fill in the relevant details (see Figure A-12). Your contacts will appear in the Contacts part of the navigation pane located on the left side of the main screen.

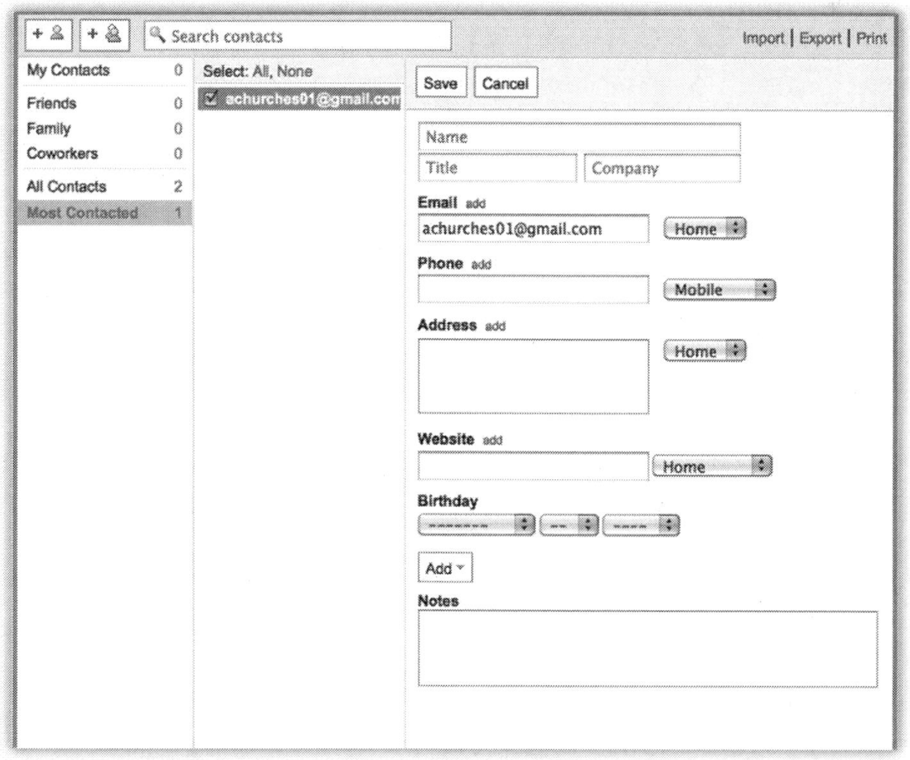

Figure A-12 *Contact information sheet*

Other Things to Think About

Following are some general concepts for email. Not all emails are safe. Some emails contain viruses and malware. Both of these can damage your computer, and can put your personal information at risk. If you don't know who a message is from, it's a good idea to not open it. It's much better to just delete it.

Consider who you give your email address to. Sometimes ticking the box on web sites to receive updates and news adds you to email lists that are used to send out spam messages. Spam can become very annoying and fill up your email in-box quickly. Think before you send an email. Sometimes you can send a message in a moment of haste that you will regret later.

Email is fast and you can write as little or much as you want. But it only takes seconds to add a subject line and a greeting. Consistently doing this can change a message from being abrupt and even rude to a polite request. It's worth the investment.

The bigger the file you attach, the longer it is going to take to send and receive. Some email services also have a limit to the size of files you can send. Consider the size of the files and images you attach. You can use a compression utility such as Stuff-It to create ZIP files—A reduced file size format for sending large attachments.

If it's not nice, don't send it. If you receive an email about something that you or others would feel uncomfortable with, don't send it on. Delete it.

Summary

- In this appendix, you used Gmail to create an email account. You can use this account to send and receive email.

- You can add a custom signature to your emails that contains relevant contact information.

- You have looked at how to compose an email and what the different parts of an email are.

- Email will allow you to communicate with friends, coworkers, business associates, and organizations anywhere in the world.

- Using web-based email systems, such as Gmail, Hotmail, or Yahoo! mail, allow you to access your email from anywhere that has an Internet connection. This is perfect for travelers, students, and just about anyone else.

Questions to Ask

- Is my account name suitable? Does it portray me in the best light?

- Is my personal password strong enough to prevent people from accessing my email account?

- Who am I going to give my email address to?

- Should I tick the box that says I would like to receive updates and newsletters from web sites?

- Should I open an email from someone I don't know?

Resources

Google's approach to email—

http://mail.google.com/mail/help/intl/en/about_whatsnew.html

Learn the NET: email from About.com—

www.learnthenet.com/english/section/email.html

Email Basics GCF LearnFree.org—www.gcflearnfree.org/Computer/Topic.aspx?id=19

A list of tutorials on the most popular email programs—www.freeemailtutorials.com

Email basics for beginners—

http://netforbeginners.about.com/od/email/Email_Tutorials_and_Articles_Start_Here.htm

Mediacollege.com basics for email—www.mediacollege.com/internet/email

# Glossary

A

Alphanumeric is a password that contains numbers and letters.

Attachment is a file or image that has been attached to an email message.

B

BCC: is an abbreviation for blind carbon copy. This is a hidden recipient of the message you are sending. People receiving this message will not be able to see anyone else who has been included in the BCC field.

Blog is a contraction of the term *web log*. A blog is an online application that allows users to post (or load) text, images, and other materials to their sites. Other readers may also be given permission to leave comments.

Blogger has a twofold meaning. A blogger is a person who writes a blog and is also the name of Google's free blogging tool.

Body is the main part of an email where you add your message. It is equivalent to the written letter in a conventional mail system.

Bookmarking is recording the web address (URL) and title of a web page for future reference. Social bookmarking allows you to share these bookmarks.

Boolean searches are searches that use Boolean search operators AND, OR, or NOT to refine a search. For example, "dogs" AND "cats" will search for pages containing both keywords cats and dogs.

Broadband is a fast Internet connection often using DSL, ADSL, ADSL2, or cable connections. The fast rate of information transfer means that this is suitable (in most cases) for audio and videoconferencing. As a general rule, the faster your connection is, the better the quality of the sound or picture you receive will be.

C

CC: stands for carbon copy. This is the field in an email where you put the secondary recipients to the message.

Chat is transferring written or typed messages between computers. For example, in Skype, the chat window allows you to transfer files as well.

Client is the software that allows you to connect to the Skype server and communicate with other people who are online at the same time. You will have to download and install the Skype client to be able to use this tool.

Client-based email is where you have a client or program installed on your computer that connects to the online email server. The client downloads the messages and stores them on the computer and uploads messages you are sending to the email server. Using a client allows you to always have access to your messages, but only on the computer your have installed the client on. You need to be online to send and receive messages, but you can construct messages offline.

Comments are voice or text comments that you add to your VoiceThread as you are creating it. Other people can add comments to your threads using voice, text, or web camera. These usually have to be moderated.

Cyberbullying is the process of attacking or bullying a person using electronic mediums such as email, instant messaging, discussion boards, cell phones, and so on.

D

Dial-up is a slow-speed connection to the Internet using a modem. Because the transfer rate of information is very low, dial-up is unsuitable for audio or videoconferencing.

Discussion boards are web spaces where users can post or write comments. They can be restricted to only members of the space or open to the public. Many discussions boards or forums are moderated.

Doodler is a drawing tool that you can use on your VoiceThreads.

Download is to take a file, such as a photograph or video, from the web site and save it on to you computer.

E

Email is the abbreviation for electronic mail. Email can be as simple as plain text containing only text or more sophisticated messages containing images, video, and even attached files.

Export is saving your VoiceThread as a file on your computer before playback through your iPod, computer, and so on.

Extensions are add-ons to your web browser that allow you to perform specific jobs or tasks. For example, the Delicious extension adds buttons to the browser toolbar that allow you to bookmark pages and go directly to your social bookmarking account.

F

Feed aggregator is a utility or tool that allows you to collect together your RSS feeds in one place and view updates, save interesting posts, and subscribe to and manage your news and information sources. These can either be online tools, such as bloglines (www.bloglines.com) or Google reader (www.google.com/reader), or software installed on your computer such as Feedreader or Flock.

Feeds are online resources such as blogs, web pages, Twitter, and so on that a user can subscribe to in a feed aggregator.

File format describes the way a document, image, or file is saved. Usually each tool saves in its own file format. For example, Microsoft Word will save in the .doc format. OpenOffice Writer will save files in the open document format, or .odf. This can sometimes cause issues of compatibility between different tools.

Firewall is a piece of software (or a physical device or machine in organizations) that controls connections into and out of your computer. Firewalls are an essential tool for keeping safe.

Flaming is when a person publicly attacks or "outs" another person. This can often be a series of posts or comments using discussion boards, forums, chatrooms, or instant messaging.

Flickr is the media-sharing web site located at www.flickr.com.

Followers are people who subscribe to your Twitter posts. People following your blog are usually described as subscribers, and those who follow you on a social network are friends.

From: This is a field located in the head of an email message that shows who the author of the message is.

G

Gmail is a free web-based email service provided by Google.

Grooming is a technique used by predators to select and prepare a person for meeting the predator. It involves building a degree of trust between the victim and the predator.

H

Head is the part of an email message that contains the address of the recipients, the subject line, and attachments. This is the equivalent of the envelope in a conventional letter.

Hits is the term used to describe the number of results from a search.

Hotmail is a free web-based email service provided by Microsoft. You will need to create a Windows Live ID to set up a Hotmail account.

J

JPG is an abbreviation for Joint Photographic Experts Group. JPG (pronounced jay-peg) is the most common image file format. Most cameras and scanners will save pictures into this format or type.

K

Keyword(s) are significant words used to describe or categorize searches or tags.

M

Malware is a term used to describe malicious software. This can include viruses, trojans, adware, spyware, and so on.

MB is an abbreviation for megabyte, which is a measure of the size of a file. A megabyte is 1024 Kb, or kilobytes, of data. 1024 MB of data makes a gigabyte, or GB.

Microblogging is a Web 2.0 tool that allows the user to post short (up to 140 characters long) updates and messages to either a public or private audience.

Moderate is when comments left by blog readers are checked by the blog owner or moderator before they are made public.

Moderating is the process where you approve the comments that have been left on your VoiceThread by other viewers. Approved comments can be listened to or viewed by other visitors to your site.

Moderation is the process of approving comments or posts by a moderator. Once approved, other users can see them.

O

Offline is when your Internet connection is inactive or switched off.

Online means that the application or tool must be accessed through the Internet. Some companies such as Google are making their tools available offline. Documents can be created and worked on offline (without connecting to the Internet) and then updated when you connect later.

Open Source Software is software often produced by a community of developers that is freely available for use and often for distribution. Open Source Software can be modified as the source code is open to view and modify.

P

PageRank is how Google ranks web pages. The higher the PageRank, the more important the page is. The pages with the highest PageRank appear first in a search.

Phishing is a technique used to gain personal and private information. Usually phishing occurs when you receive an email from an apparently legitimate source asking you to provide information or to link to a web site to update your personal information. The information is collected (such as bank account or credit card details) and then used by the email or web site authors.

Photostream is a term used to describe the pictures uploaded by a user.

Piracy is the illegal copying and/or distribution of copyrighted materials. This can include music, images, movies, television programs, written works, and other intellectual property.

Pixel is a dot of a single color within an image. Most images are several megapixels, which means the image is made up of several million dots. An image that is 1024 pixels wide by 768 pixels in height (this is the size of the average computer screen) is about ¾ of a megabyte or 750 kilobytes in size.

Post is where an entry or update in your blog published.

Posts are comments, statements, articles, or presentations published by a user. The term *post* covers blog entries (see Chapter 7), short messages using tools such as Twitter (see Chapter 6), email messages to discussion boards or forums, or updates on a social networking site (see Chapter 8).

Predator is a person using the Internet and online social mediums to groom, stalk, and make contact with a goal of sexual exploitation.

Presentation tools are tools that allow the user to enter information and present it in a suitable format, usually a slideshow-style format. Examples of this include StarOffice and OpenOffice Impress, Apple Keynote, and Microsoft PowerPoint.

Productivity tools is the term used to describe work-related tools such as word processors, spreadsheets, presentation tools, and so on. Some good offline examples of productivity suites include Apple iWork, Microsoft Office, Sun's StarOffice, and the open source OpenOffice 3.0. There are also many online productivity suites, including Google Documents and Zoho Documents.

Profile is the personal information you have entered in social networking (see Chapter 8) and other sites.

Protected is where only followers you have approved and accepted can see your posts or tweets.

Public timeline is publicly viewable messages that are not protected.

R

RSS is an abbreviation for Really Simple Syndication. RSS is a tool that allows you to subscribe to various online feeds and receive notification when these are updated.

RSS aggregator is a tool that allows you to subscribe to the updates from blogs you follow. The aggregator can be an online tool, such as bloglines, or a tool installed on your computer, such as Feedreader.

S

Search engine is a database connected to the Web that allows the user to locate online resources based on words and phrases entered into the search field. Examples of search engines include Google, Yahoo!, MetaCrawler, Dogpile, and so on.

Server is a central computer that you access. This can be the computer that collects and sends out your email messages. The server routes the messages you send via a series of steps to the server that is hosting the message recipient's email account and from there to the message recipient. It can be the computer hosting your Flickr pictures, Twitter account, VoiceThread presentations, and so on.

Set is a group of images that are related in some way. Using sets makes organizing images simple and manageable.

Signature is a text element that is added to an email message usually containing the email author's contact details. This is automatically added to the end of most email messages.

Slide show is a progression of images and text used to convey a message.

Spam is unsolicited or unrequested email often sent out by fictitious companies. Spam is a huge issue creating vast email traffic and causing great annoyance.

Spreadsheets are tools that allow the user to enter, format, and process data using columns, rows, formulas, and equations. Examples are Microsoft Excel, StarOffice Calc, OpenOffice Calc, and Apple's Numbers.

Subject is a field where you indicate what the message is about. It is considered bad manners to not have a subject line in an email message. Subject lines make it easier to manage messages and quickly sort through them.

T

Tags are keywords used to classify your blog posts, bookmarks, and so on. Users will often use tags or keywords to sort or search through all of your posts.

To: is the key address field where you put the email address of the primary recipient of the message. You must have a primary recipient in an email message.

Tweet is a popular name for the user's posts on the microblogging tool Twitter.

Twitter is a microblogging tool that allows you to aggregate other Twitter feeds and manage your feeds and posts.

U

Upload is taking a file, such as a document, spreadsheet, music file, picture, or video, and sending it to your online service such as Flickr, VoiceThread, email message, and so on.

URL stands for Universal Resource Locater. A URL is the web address of a page or online resource. For example, the address www.cnn.com is the URL or web address of the CNN television channel.

V

VoIP stands for Video and Voice over Internet Protocol. Essentially, this is a set of rules that allow you to use your computer and Internet connection to communicate with people who also have the VoIP client active.

W

Web 2.0 is a term used to describe web pages and sites that allow users to add content as well as read them. Web 2.0 is also called the read/write web.

Web-based email are email accounts where the messages are stored on an email server on the Internet, such as Hotmail or gmail. These messages can be accessed anywhere you have Internet access. However, if you do not have Internet access, you cannot gain access to your messages.

Web browser is a program that allows you to surf the Internet. The most common web browsers are Microsoft's Internet Explorer, Mozilla's Firefox, and Apple's Safari.

Word processors are tools that allow users to enter and format text into documents. Some examples are Microsoft Word, StarOffice Writer, OpenOffice Writer, and Apple's Pages.

WordPress is a company that hosts blogs and provides brilliant blog hosting software.

WYSIWYG is an abbreviation for What You See Is What You Get. This phrase describes tools that let you enter text and format it in the style that it will appear on the screen or when it is printed out. A word processor such as Microsoft Word or Apple's Pages is described as being a WYSIWYG word processor. With a WYSIWYG editor, you do not need to know any code, like HTML, JavaScript, and such, to produce web pages.

Index

C

D

I

J

K

L

M

Y

Z